Carmel of the Little Flower of Jesus
The Beautiful Garden

Michael J. Valaik

Michael J. Valaik
2020

First Printing: 2020

ISBN: 978-0-578-71551-3

Carmel of the Little Flower of Jesus
75 Carmel Road
Buffalo, NY 14216

https://www.buffalocarmel.org/

Printed in the United States of America

To the Carmelites of Buffalo, living and past.

Contents

Acknowledgements

This book stems from my love for the Carmelites of Buffalo. It started as a young boy and continues to this day. The Sisters shaped me and my life in profound ways. In a small measure, I try to give back here to those that give all to God.

Since the first moment that the Prioress agreed to this book for the monastery's centenary celebration, the Holy Spirit guided the project. Although based on discussions with the Sisters, historical records, and other materials, often parts fell into place, ideas came, and words ended up on the page. The Sisters asked the Holy Spirit to guide me, and He did. That said, any errors or mistakes are mine alone.

Debbie Horvath and Madeline Barnas got this project to the finish line and turned the draft into a book. Many thanks to them.

Finally, like all my endeavors, Susan's love and wisdom provides the light. I remain ever grateful to her.

Prologue

"To be thy spouse, O Jesus, to be a Carmelite, and in union with Thee, to be the mother of souls."

St. Therese of Lisieux

In 1897, a young Carmelite died an obscure death in a cloistered monastery in Lisieux, France. St. Therese lived only twenty-four years. Before her death, she begged God to raise up an army of souls who would follow her Little Way of spiritual childhood. This Little Way—to love God and share His love with others through our ordinary, everyday actions—soon spread like fire, and its impact still resonates today. While the Little Flower lay dying in France, Carmelites in Mexico faced persecution and exile.

***

Founded in 1920, the Carmel of Buffalo celebrates its centenary this year.

The chapel, built and dedicated as a shrine to the Little Flower, stands at the forefront both visible and open to the public. The exterior grounds lend beauty and peace to this north Buffalo neighborhood. People passing by might see the Extern Sisters, in their distinct brown and white garb, tending the grounds, while the monastery remains a mystery to most. The cloister lies behind the twelve-foot, white walls where beautiful gardens grow around devotional shrines in honor of Christ, the Blessed Virgin Mary, and various saints. Flowers, trees, and a pond paint a scene, while birds create the melody. In accord with Church law and the constitutions of their Order, the public never sees the cloister Sisters and the interior garden where they retreat to pray. Although peace and tranquility envelop the Carmel of Buffalo today, that stands in contrast to its surroundings.

After the Erie Canal opened in 1825, Buffalo thrived and became the ninth most populous city in the United States. The Canal created a navigable water route from the Atlantic Ocean in New York City to the Great Lakes, connecting the eastern United States with the growing western interior. Buffalo still stood strong as a leading industrial city in 1920 when the monastery was founded, but the city slowly declined starting in the 1970s. And today, like a lot of cities, crime and violence occur all too regularly in Buffalo. The monastery's history also included violent events in the early 1900s, as revolutionary forces in Mexico battled for government control. Religious were frequent targets, including Mother Mary Elias of the Blessed Sacrament, a nun in the Carmelite Monastery of Queretaro.

Mother Elias ultimately fled Mexico, came to the United States, and settled in Grand Rapids, Michigan. But before her exile, revolutionaries took her prisoner and put her before a firing squad. Facing her executioners, she fervently prayed to the French Carmelite Sr. Therese of Lisieux, before the Little Flower had become well-known. Her prayer vowed that, if spared, Mother Elias would establish a new Carmelite monastery in Therese's name. Shots were fired, but miraculously Mother Elias lived, escaped, and founded the Carmel of the Little Flower of Jesus in St. Therese's honor.

That spiritual connection between the Little Flower and Mother Elias can still be felt in the chapel today. To hear the Carmelite Sisters in song, a clear message emerges—this place and these prayers are different. An intense love for God motivates those who enter Carmel with a genuine call. Their love becomes a lifelong journey to seek God in a Community of like-minded Sisters, originally intended by their Foundress to number thirteen like Jesus and His apostles. The Sisters live, pray, and die at the monastery. They wake each morning at 5:15 a.m., pray seven times a day, observe the Fast of the Order for seven months of the year, abstain perpetually from meat, and work generously. They garden, make meals, clean, sew, and do many other tasks. The Sisters observe the strict silence for most of each day, and the Great (complete) Silence at night. The silence helps the Sisters find God in a more profound way.

Unlike most Catholic Orders, the Discalced Carmelites live a cloistered life, which means they do not participate in society. St. Teresa of Avila, whom the Carmelites refer to as "our Holy Mother," reformed the Order and described monastic life in *The Way of Perfection* (1566). Writing shortly after the Council of Trent (1545-1563), St. Teresa led the Order back to the strictness of the primitive

x

Carmelite Rule. She adopted the specific mission to pray for priests. Because priests spread the Faith and shepherd the flock on the front lines, St. Teresa feared they might become *of* the world due to living *in* the world. Carmel's mission remains the same today.

Almost five hundred years after St. Teresa of Avila's time, Carmelite life stands athwart popular culture. Carmelites vow to be chaste, poor, and obedient, and commit their whole lives to God. We lead hurried lives and struggle to find time for God. Many people reject religion altogether. No one discusses chastity, poverty, or obedience, let alone vows to live this way. But brave women at the Carmel of Buffalo do, leaving our world forever. As a result of these differences, we might dismiss the monastery as a world apart—some kind of different life, meant for different people. That conclusion, however, is too simplistic.

I went to the Carmel of Buffalo at seven years old to be an altar boy in 1972. My family lived on Parkside Avenue, a few doors down from St. Rose of Lima grammar school. St. Rose typically assigned altar boys for weekday Mass at the monastery, once every two months, for a week at a time. Tough duty for a young boy, as Mass began at 7:30 a.m. But the monastery intrigued me from the start, primarily because I met an Extern Sister named Sister Mary Joseph.

Extern Sisters do not live in the strict enclosure of the monastery, but rather serve as liaison between the cloister and the world. In my day, Sr. Mary Joseph trained the altar boys. A former Naval Officer in World War II, she instilled discipline and attention to detail, but with a loving hand. For reasons I did not yet understand, she demanded perfection, as if God watched each altar boy during Mass. She gently challenged me to do better. Sr. Mary Joseph soon asked me to serve Mass on Sundays and stay after for breakfast. I started to go weekdays when not assigned, special feast days, and many other occasions. It helped that my older brother Dan often went with me. After countless Masses and time spent with the Sisters, I formed a lasting bond such that when I left for college in 1983, I knew two things with complete certainty: Buffalo would never be home again, but Carmel would always be home.

Trips back to Buffalo after college to see my parents grew infrequent as I deployed to Europe, Liberia, and the Gulf War as a U.S. Marine. Attending Mass while deployed overseas as a Marine though, my thoughts and prayers always drifted back to the monastery and the Sisters. It was as if time and distance did not matter because my connection to the Carmelites remained palpable. Like a gravitational pull, I longed to go home spiritually to the place and people that nurtured my soul. And yet despite this strong connection, mystery still surrounded the monastery. The nuns knelt behind the iron grate during Mass, completely out of sight. I had never met a cloistered sister my entire life, and yet that gut feeling that the monastery would always be home had proven correct. But why?

Fifty-three, with four children grown and gone, I contacted the Prioress and offered to write a book in celebration of the monastery's centenary year, hoping to answer that question. After she agreed, what unfolded revealed much more than I imagined. Indeed, Carmel's connection, not just to me but to our world, emerged in a number of ways. First, Carmelites do not enter the cloister simply for their own salvation. They answer God's call to save all souls and to spend themselves for His glory as a response of love to Love. Second, their mission to pray for priests, something more vital to the Church today than at any point, remains at the core of their vocation. Finally, those cloistered Sisters may leave our world, but they keenly understand the secular world around them and work tirelessly so that we will see Christ's love as the answer.

In the end, the Carmel of Buffalo's story reveals a beautiful pattern—from the world into the cloister as a woman seeks her vocation, and then from the cloister back out into the world through the Sisters' prayer and sacrifice. The second part (from the monastery back to the world) remains mysterious, in part because we fail to understand the Carmelite's vocation and hear the Sisters' prayers. Without ever breaking silence, the Carmelites prayerfully "shout out" to reach us and hope we feel their love. If we could see and feel the connection between the monastery and us, we too might draw closer to God and begin to see things through a new lens of love.

This book celebrates the Carmel of the Little Flower of Jesus—its foundation, its struggles, the unwavering faith, but most of all the

Sisters' love. Part One is titled "The Beautiful Garden," and it recounts the history of Carmel's beginnings in Buffalo, its founders, and the early years. Part Two is titled "The Interior Garden," and it explores who is drawn to this life of prayer, its beauty, and stories of some of the Carmelites that have called the monastery home. Part Three is "The Fruits of the Garden," which explains how we might share in the good that flows from the monastery.

Although we never see their faces, the reader hopefully will perceive the Carmelites' faces here, and in that sense the book is more akin to a portrait than a history. Not a sophisticated explanation of Carmelite spirituality in any way, my hope is to unwrap some of the mystery and engender a deep appreciation for Carmel's impact in our world. To use a phrase, these few Sisters have been "punching well above their weight" in Buffalo and beyond for one hundred years, imploring the Little Flower to shower roses on us.

We should be grateful, above all else!

I
THE BEAUTIFUL GARDEN

1

Seedlings

I have led you into the land of Carmel to eat the fruit and good things thereof.

Jeremiah 2:7

This biblical verse sits high on the wall in the choir where the Sisters attend Mass and pray the Divine Office as a constant reminder of the good that comes from a vocation to Carmel. The Carmelite Order traces its roots back to the prophet Elijah, who sought God on the biblical Carmel, a high hill in Palestine, 900 years before Christ. Shortly after the American Revolutionary War in 1790, four nuns left Belgium and established the first Carmelite cloister in Port Tobacco, Maryland, later moving to Baltimore in 1831. These Carmelite women formed the first Roman Catholic convent in the United States, which served as the foundation for many more Carmelite monasteries. This same pioneering spirit led to the formation of the Carmel of the Little Flower of Jesus in Buffalo.

Founding a Carmelite monastery requires more than simply building a physical structure. Although necessary, the structure purposefully veils the Sisters from the peering eyes of the world. If the world could see, the monastery would appear as a beautiful garden of souls. Carmel literally means "Beautiful Garden." Gardens begin when seedlings grow roots in the soil. Water and sun provide nourishment, and soon the seedling sprouts. With proper nurturing and care, the seedling grows into a strong plant. Carmel cultivates vocations like seedlings that form in chosen souls. Prayer, community life, and the observance of the Carmelite Rule nourish these souls and guide their quest towards perfect union with God. These seedlings eventually become a garden dedicated to the Lord. The specific seedlings for the foundation of the Carmel of Buffalo began in the hearts and souls of two courageous Carmelites.

***

Therese Martin, more popularly known as St. Therese of Lisieux, was born in Normandy, France in 1873. She lost her mother at age four, and she lamented in her autobiography that: "After Mamma's death, my naturally happy disposition deserted me. I who had been so lively and open became now a shy, quiet, over-sensitive little girl." Therese attended the Abbey school in Lisieux, and because she was already advanced in her studies, the school placed Therese with older girls who did not accept this younger, intelligent girl. Therese withdrew and looked at her loneliness as an opportunity to draw closer to God. She read about saints like Joan of Arc and aspired to sanctity as well. Unlike Joan of Arc, Therese knew her glory would not be in this life, but in the Life to come.

Therese's older sister Pauline had already entered the Carmelite monastery in Lisieux by the time Therese made her First Holy Communion. Soon thereafter, her sister Marie followed Pauline into Carmel. Throughout her childhood, Therese suffered bouts of sickness and as a result lacked the confidence to pursue a vocation. She naturally turned to the Lord and His Mother for help, and God granted her a grace of inner healing on Christmas Eve of 1886. She wrote, "I had recovered the strength of mind which I lost at four and a half, and I recovered it for good. In a single instant our Lord brought about the change which I had tried vainly to achieve for ten years ... Our Lord newly-born, turned this darkness of mine into a flood of light."

Therese now yearned to enter the monastery. But because she was so young, Therese needed the permission of the Bishop to enter Carmel. Therese went to Bayeux and met with the Bishop, but he refused. Undeterred, Therese and her father went to Rome with the hope of meeting Pope Leo XIII. The day that Therese visited the Vatican, November 20, 1887, the authorities told her specifically not to address the Pope if they met. Nonetheless, when the Pope received the pilgrims from Lisieux, Therese did speak, saying "Holy Father, I want to ask you a great favor. In honor of your jubilee, let me enter Carmel at fifteen." Before Pope Leo responded, the Vicar General of Bayeux told the Pope that the proper authorities already had considered her case. The Pope responded: "Very well, my child, do what your superiors tell you." Therese persisted, begging, "Holy Father, if you said yes, everyone will agree." The Pope then very deliberately told her: "If God wants you to enter, you will." Shortly after in January 1888, the Bishop granted Therese permission to enter Carmel of Lisieux to begin life as a Carmelite. She was only fifteen.

Although the Little Flower's time at Carmel was rather short, spanning only nine years, the significance of her vocation is still being measured today because of the tremendous impact her Little Way has had on subsequent generations. Pauline (Mother Agnes of Jesus) became the Prioress in 1893, and Therese became the assistant Novice Mistress, helping with the formation of the young postulants and novices. Therese did everything to guide the novices in her Little Way. She strove to make them understand that love should inspire all our actions, and she wrote: "You know well enough that our Lord does not look so much at the greatness of our actions, nor even at their difficulty, but at the love with which we do them ... Love is the only thing we should strive for. That is why we should prefer the action we can do with greater love, whether it is 'harder' or 'easier.'"

Therese taught the novices that spiritual perfection required taking their eyes off of themselves and focusing entirely on their Beloved. When a novice commented that she still had "so much she had *to acquire*" in the spiritual life, Therese responded: "Rather, *to lose*! Jesus will fill your soul to the degree that you rid it of imperfections ... You want to climb the mountain, while God wants you to descend it. He is waiting for you in the fruitful valley of humility."

On Holy Thursday 1896, Therese coughed up blood, an early indication of tuberculosis. Her illness became worse during the bitter winter of 1896-97. As death drew closer, Therese began to appreciate the significance of her Little Way and its potential to reach well beyond Lisieux. She asked Mother Agnes to assemble her papers and writings for future generations. And then Therese predicted what was to come after her death: "I feel that my mission is soon to begin, to make others love God as I do, to teach others my Little Way. I will spend my heaven doing good upon earth ... After my death, I will let fall a shower of roses." Therese entered into Eternal Life on September 30, 1897.

Instead of the typical circular letter, which Carmels compose to share a deceased Sister's life story with other monasteries, Mother Agnes fulfilled Therese's request and sent instead what became her autobiographical account titled "The Story of a Soul." Soon the other monasteries passed along Therese's story to friends and acquaintances, and the Little Way spread rapidly. Stories of cures, miracles, and the Little Flower's amazing power to shower roses followed. Pope Pius XI stated in the Bull of St. Therese's Canonization: "Without going beyond the common order of things in her way of life, she followed and fulfilled her vocation with such alacrity, generosity and constancy that she reached a heroic degree of virtue." All can identify with her Little Way because we too can be virtuous "without going beyond the common order of things."

St. Therese wrote, "You want a means of reaching perfection. I know of only one: love." The Little Flower's influence touched another Carmelite soul, the second seedling in Carmel of the Little Flower of Jesus's foundation, Mother Mary Elias of the Blessed Sacrament.

***

Born Maria Elana Thierry in Mexico City on the Feast of the Assumption in 1879, she was the third youngest of seventeen children. Like St. Therese, her mother died while she was still a child, and Maria struggled to find her place. Although her exceptional gifts for organization and discipline made Maria a successful teacher, she felt Our Lord drawing her to a deeper intimacy with Himself. After a period of discernment, she applied to the Carmel in Mexico City. Because of political unrest, the Community dispensed with the normal stage of postulancy and allowed Maria to enter the Novitiate right away with the reception of the Habit. A few years later Mother Elias left Mexico City with two other Sisters to restore the Carmel of Queretaro.

After Mexico declared its independence from Spain in 1810, the Carmel of Queretaro faced persecution and hardship amid the revolutionary environment. By the mid-nineteenth century, the Sisters feared for their lives and had to leave the monastery. When the Religious cannot live the monastic life in the monastery, they seek "exclaustration," which is official authorization for those bound by perpetual vows to reside outside of the monastery. The Carmel of Queretaro faced this dilemma on May 14, 1867, which was recorded in an eyewitness account:

> They (the Carmelites) left two-by-two with veils
> lowered. Arriving at the portress' entrance they,

crying, embraced the Prioress, prostrated themselves, kissed the lintel of the door and were received by pious people or those known to be of high society. There was only one carriage, which I now suppose would have been for the Reverend Mother Prioress. They left nevermore to return.

Some forty years later, only one of the Carmelites that left Queretaro remained. Elderly and blind, Mother Euphrosina still recited the Divine Office, prayed in complete solitude, and kept the Faith in hope that one day God would restore her beloved monastery. God answered these prayers in December 1908, when Mothers Teresa Maria ("Teresita"), Mary Bernard, and Mary Elias left Mexico City to restore the Community. Sr. Isabel of the Most Holy Trinity recorded this event in the chronicles,[1] "For Mother Euphrosina the years of living in exile did not lessen in her the love of all that is in our Holy Rule and the faithful observance of it. Her heart overflowing with intense joy, she surrendered herself into the hands of her new Prioress and comported herself as a Carmelite Novice. Her example was edifying beyond all measure." Mother Euphrosina died one month later on January 19, 1909, her earthly mission complete, and the Community was canonically established as a new foundation on the Feast of Our Lady of Guadalupe in December 1909.

But the persecution continued, and the attacks on Religious worsened after the revolutionary Francisco Madero declared war on President Dias in 1910. The revolutionaries executed priests and drove more Religious from their monasteries. They stole, defaced, and destroyed Catholic devotional articles and valuable sacred artifacts. Soldiers profaned churches, and prostitutes wore priestly vestments as a mockery. The Blessed Sacrament was even fed to horses. While these abominations continued, the Religious could not easily flee because the depreciation of the peso made travel too expensive.

Elected Prioress at the young age of thirty-three, Mother Elias did not falter in the face of these trials. Instead, she prepared for the day

---

[1] Carmelite monasteries record their histories in type-written accounts, which include significant events in the Community, such as visits from the Father General of the Order, the Bishop, as well as other noteworthy events. These histories are referred to as the chronicles.

when her Sisters might need to flee. She started to collect secular clothes, wigs, and shoes for disguises, hiding these items in the monastery attic. When the Bishop of Queretaro died in May 1914, the Carmelites fled the monastery again. Each Sister, still dressed in the habit underneath and a secular outfit on the outside, disappeared into the local community. A month later, on June 13, 1914, Mother Elias formally resigned as Prioress and left Queretaro for Aguascalientes with some of her Sisters to find safety. The next day, Queretaro fell to the revolutionaries. Mother Elias's respite from the chaos, however, was short-lived, as Poncho Villa soon took the town of Aguascalientes and confiscated the house where Mother and her Sisters were living. Once again, the nuns dissolved into the community in secular disguises.

One day, as Mother begged for bread, she saw horses carrying beautiful religious statues and other devotional items to the town square. Inquiring why, Mother learned that the revolutionaries planned to burn these sacred objects. Mother sprang into action and implored the Governor to reverse the impending sacrilege. Appearing in disguise, Mother pled with the Governor to prevent the public desecration, which he granted. But only a few weeks later, the Governor asked that the leaders of the Religious Orders appear before him to explain why they all should not be exiled from Mexico.

Weakened, tired, and hungry, Mother Elias shed her disguise and appeared as a Carmelite. When the Governor questioned her, he looked closely and said: "Madame, I think I have met you before?" "My General," Mother answered, "it is only two weeks since I came to this very place to beg your illustrious person to withdraw the order which had been given to burn the statues in the public square, and you kindly granted my request." The Governor asked why then Mother Elias appeared different, and she explained how the Sisters wore regular clothes over their habits. The Governor laughed, remarking to Mother Elias how hot and uncomfortable that must be. Mother agreed that yes, indeed, it was uncomfortable! Despite this brief moment of laughter, Mother argued her case to no avail.

The Governor ordered the Carmelites to leave Mexico forever. Mother Elias was able to persuade him to grant her sufficient time to raise money to ensure proper passage. In October 1914, Mother Elias and her Sisters were prepared to leave, but because of insufficient funds, Mother Teresita and the older professed nuns were going to stay behind. Those nuns departing took a train from Aguascalientes to Veracruz and then boarded a ship to Cuba. Arriving after a two-day sea voyage, the nuns settled in their new surroundings. But Mother Elias was aware of her responsibility as Prioress to bring the rest of her Sisters out of Mexico. Mother Elias worked with Monsignor Francis Kelley, a Jesuit in Cuba who was writing a book about the persecution of the Church in Mexico, to obtain the necessary funds to rescue the remaining nuns. She left Cuba in early December, and Msgr. Kelley arranged for a young postulant named Sister Angela to meet Mother Elias in Mexico City. As they both left Mexico City on a train, revolutionaries stopped and arrested them. Thrown into a prison camp, they shared a cell with other Catholic priests and Religious. Each night the guards questioned them and asked where other Religious were living in Mexico. Mother was particularly worried that the guards might find and confiscate the money that Msgr. Kelley had given her, but they never did.

One night, the guards called Mother Elias and Sr. Angela for another round of questioning, but they refused to answer. Their lack of cooperation drove the guards into a rage, and they ordered execution for both Sisters that same night. Led into a field and put before a firing squad on a cold December evening, Mother Elias and Sr. Angela bravely refused hoods and chose to confront their executioners face-to-face. While facing certain death, Mother Elias raised a prayer to the Little Flower, stating: "*Little Therese, if you are a saint, as some people say you are, then deliver us, and I promise to found a Monastery in your honor.*" Shots rang out. Mother Elias and Sr. Angela slumped to the ground.

In the middle of the night, Mother Elias awoke lying in the field, apparently unharmed. Surprised not to be in heaven, Mother rolled around to confirm that she was alive. Sr. Angela awoke beside her, also unharmed. Suddenly, a soldier approached them, and Mother said: "Don't shoot at us; think of our Blessed Mother! You will be punished if you do!" The soldier was frightened and told Mother that he could not help them escape, but he did point the nuns to the back edge of the property. They quickly got up and fled the prison.

Walking for a short time, they came to a road. Close to daybreak, they saw a man on a horse approaching. With their fate now in God's hands, the man asked, "What are two women doing out here on this road at this hour?" Mother Elias wanted to avoid his question, but she replied, "We just escaped from prison." The man said, "Well then, I am a Priest, and I ride to the prison each morning to spend time with those souls going to their execution." Mother Elias and Sr. Angela were speechless at this blessing of Diving Providence. He offered them his horse (one of the only things on earth Mother Elias was afraid of), and confidently said the horse knew his way directly to the train depot. Sure enough, Mother Elias and Sr. Angela took the horse all the way to the depot and boarded the next train to Mexico City.

When they arrived Christmas Eve day, Mother Elias and Sr. Angela went directly to the Shrine of Our Lady of Guadalupe, knelt at the door of the Basilica, and proceeded all the way to the sanctuary on their knees in thanksgiving. Exhausted from the ordeal, the Sisters checked into an English hotel because it was the safest place to rest. Both Mother Elias and Sr. Angela noticed separately that their garments had holes and blood stains, but no wounds of any kind. The Little Flower had indeed interceded! After they rested on Christmas day, Mother Elias and Sr. Angela finally returned to Aguascalientes the next day and met Mother Teresita and the remaining Sisters. Joy overwhelmed them.

Mother Elias safely left Mexico with the remaining Sisters, and their travels to find a new monastic home continued throughout 1915 between Cuba, New Orleans, and Chicago. The Community eventually settled in Grand Rapids, Michigan. On February 2, 1916, the Carmelite monastery of Queretaro, Mexico, reformed officially in Grand Rapids under the title of Our Lady of Guadalupe. Grand Rapids Carmel recently celebrated its 100th anniversary in 2016.[2] The transition for the Mexican Sisters in Grand Rapids was hard. The cold climate, foreign language, and other difficulties made it challenging to establish the new

---

[2] The Carmelites of Buffalo are grateful to the Sisters of Grand Rapids because the story of Mother Elias's struggles in Mexico is largely taken from Grand Rapids' records and Mother's own accounts. When Mother Elias first arrived in Grand Rapids, the Bishop asked her to record these events because there was little understanding of the persecution of the Church in Mexico. Mother Elias's papers remain at Grand Rapids to this day.

10

monastery. Despite these trials, Mother Elias began to think about her promise made to the Little Flower before the firing squad.

The Grand Rapids Community received correspondence from Mother Gabriel of the St. Louis Carmel that discussed the possibility of a new foundation in Buffalo, New York. Bishop Turner, a native of Ireland and professor of philosophy at the Catholic University of America, became Bishop of Buffalo on April 10, 1919, and he wanted a Carmelite monastery in the diocese. Monsignor Nelson Baker, the Vicar General of the diocese and another instrumental figure, also wanted a Carmelite monastery in Buffalo. When the time came for the foundation to be made, it was not Mother Gabriel who received permission from her Bishop to go to Buffalo, but Mother Elias.

On April 12, 1920, Mother Mary Elias of the Blessed Sacrament arrived in Buffalo, along with Sister Mary of St. John of the Cross (later, Mother St. John) and Sister Anna of St. Bartholomew (later, foundress of the Detroit and Kansas City Carmels). They proceeded to St. Joseph's Old Cathedral, but it was too late for Mass. The Sisters then went to call on Bishop Turner, but much to her embarrassment, Mother Elias had forgotten the customary papers from the Grand Rapids Diocese. Bishop Turner still graciously welcomed them, and the nuns received His Excellency's blessing.

But after meeting the Bishop, the nuns got lost. Exhausted from the long journey and confused in their new surroundings, they took a wrong turn when leaving the chancery. After a few miles the nuns realized their error, while a car slowly approached, and much to their surprise, Msgr. Baker asked, "What are you doing here?" Mother explained what had happened, and Msgr. Baker guided them to their new monastery on Cottage Street. Though the house was bare, lacking even running water, the Sisters ate their bread that night with gratitude to God in their hearts. Msgr. Baker came the next day with news that Bishop Turner had arranged for the nuns to stay with the Sisters of St. Joseph until the new monastery was properly completed.

The Carmel of Buffalo formally opened a few days later, April 24, 1920, when Bishop Turner celebrated Mass for the Community at 49 Cottage Street.

From the very outset, the Little Flower's presence in the new monastery was evident. The local Catholics responded to her presence, and often brought the sick to be blessed with her relics. Most people welcomed the Carmelites, but others criticized their way of life, the strict nature of the cloister, and the "foreign" group of Mexican Sisters. To improve the relationship with the local community, Father Crimmen[3] organized public novenas, and the crowds soon outgrew the small chapel. The monastery, still in its infancy, already needed a larger structure. Privacy also became an issue because when the Sisters went out into the cloister garden, peering eyes from the higher buildings could easily observe them.

Amongst these growing pains, vocations increased under Mother Elias's guidance. Her strong, straightforward character as well as her attractive, magnanimous spirit appealed to the new Sisters and made them aspire to be fervent Carmelites. The other Mexican Sisters also provided a shining example by their generous labor and heroic sacrifice. Much older than the postulants, the Mexican Sisters would sew until 2 a.m. and then rise at 4:30 a.m. for mental prayer. In awe, the postulants readily embraced the austerities of Carmel with humility and generosity in light of the beautiful example they witnessed.

However, Mother Elias's time at the Carmel of Buffalo soon came to an end. Although it was surprising that a new foundation like Buffalo would be asked to form yet another monastery, that is exactly what happened. Father Edmund F. Gibbons, pastor of St. Teresa's Church on Seneca Street in Buffalo, became Bishop of Albany. He wanted a Carmelite monastery in his new diocese too, and so he asked Mother Elias to pray about his request. Mother Elias dutifully followed Bishop Gibbon's request, even with her concerns because the Carmel of Buffalo had so recently been formed.

---

[3] Fr. George A. Crimmen was appointed as the chaplain to the Community in October of 1920. A veteran of World War I, Fr. Crimmen was in poor health, but he recovered well enough to serve as chaplain until his death in 1946. Another significant figure was Father Alphonsus Duff, O.F.M., who was appointed as the first confessor. He was a Franciscan who defended the Carmelites in the early years when they were faced with criticism from the local community. Fr. Alphonsus would serve as confessor until his death in May of 1934.

On the day following the beatification of the Little Flower, April 29, 1923, God sent a sign in the form of an abundant fragrance of roses and a palpable sense of peace over the monastery. Mother Elias knew that she must accept the will of God and move to Schenectady to form a new foundation. On August 13, 1923, she left for Schenectady, only returning once briefly in 1926. Mother Elias made many more foundations and eventually returned to her life in Grand Rapids. Although Mother Elias had a wide influence on different Carmelite monasteries, she will always be considered a member of the Carmel of Our Lady of Guadalupe of Grand Rapids.

The Carmel of Buffalo's origins and the seedlings for the monastery reflect both courage and that pioneering spirit typical of the Carmelites. The Little Flower sought the Pope's permission to enter the Carmel of Lisieux while only a child, which demonstrated great courage and her fervent desire to be a Carmelite. Mother Euphrosina single-handedly kept up the observance at the Carmel of Queretaro for forty years. She welcomed Mother Elias and the other Sisters who restored her monastery, briefly, until the persecution continued. Mother Elias begged for food in the streets, pled with the Governor to defend her Faith, and ultimately faced a firing squad. She endured untold daily hardship, and yet she persevered. Mother Elias possessed that rare combination of resolute firmness in the face of adversity, along with a loving hand to lead her flock to safety.

Mother Elias and the Carmelites of Queretaro ultimately made their journey to Buffalo after a long odyssey. But before she fled, Mother Elias and St. Therese connected. Two souls and two seedlings linked as one in a prison field. Mother Elias faced her executioners with the hope that the Little Flower would intercede on her behalf. A bond formed, one that served as the foundation of the Carmel of Buffalo and led to the dedication of the chapel on the very day of the Little Flower's canonization, May 17, 1925.

2

Roots

You are the pride of our city, and this building raised through the offerings of devoted friends, shows how Buffalo appreciates the treasure that it has in you.

Father Bernard Fuller

The Sisters moved from Cottage Street to the new monastery on April 19, 1925, two years after Mother Elias's departure for Schenectady. Mother Elias took a leap of faith leaving, and she also took with her the original Sisters who had come to Buffalo from Mexico, except one. That Sister was Mother Mary of St. John of the Cross, affectionately known as "Little Mother." Since she knew little English, the remaining Sisters feared Little Mother would be lonely. But by her death in 1949, Little Mother had become the instrumental force in the Carmel of the Little Flower of Jesus establishing its roots.

***

Born Alice Buxbaum on August 27, 1876, in London, England, Little Mother had a pleasant childhood. Her mother, a toy store owner named Isabel, and her father, jewelry merchant George Buxbaum, took her to many countries, and she spoke multiple languages at a young age. Although Alice never wanted for material things, her parents did decide she would not have one thing: her mother, a fallen-away Catholic, was adamant that Alice never be introduced to religion or even hear the name of God. When Alice saw people going to the beautiful churches in London and Paris and asked what they were doing, her parents provided no answers. As a child, Alice naturally was seeking, but no one helped guide her. One day, however, God intervened directly and revealed His presence. Alice dreamt of a Man in a long garment, wearing a crown of thorns and carrying a reed. He spoke: "You must be very good and avoid doing any evil. If you are good, you will be rewarded, but if you are bad, you will be condemned." Alice kept this dream close to her heart as a child, and as she matured at the Carmel of Buffalo, Little Mother recalled the dream often because it shaped her entire life.

14

Alice traveled with her mother to Mexico for an extended stay during her teenage years, and they settled in San Luis Potosi. On one occasion when her mother went on a trip, Alice stayed at a boarding school in the care of two devout ladies. Here, Alice encountered faith firsthand when she saw one of the ladies praying. Naturally, Alice asked what she was doing, but the lady tried to ignore Alice because her mother had forbidden such discussion. Alice persisted, and finally the lady relented and said, "I was praying."

"Praying?" she echoed. "What is that?"

"I am asking God for the things I need."

"God?" said Alice, "who is God?"

The devout mistress tried to explain in a simple way which her listener could understand.

"God," she explained, "is the One Who created you and Who gives you all you have."

"My *mother* gives me all I have," answered the child.

"Yes, but who gives it to your mother?"

"My father," answered Alice without hesitation. "My mother gets everything from my father!"

"But where does your father get it?" gently asked the mistress.

"He works for it," said Alice.

"But who gives him the health and strength to work?"

Alice was puzzled. Yes, WHO DID give her father the health and strength to work?

Then simply, gently, convincingly, the holy school mistress explained to her little charge the sweet mystery of God; and for the first time in her life, this restless heart, which ceaselessly had been reaching out for something more to satisfy it, was appeased. Thereafter, it could never be satisfied with anything less than God.

We do not know to what extent the instruction of these two women reached. One thing is certain: they taught Alice the *Hail Mary* and recommended she say it without fail every day. Alice soon persuaded the ladies to take her to Mass, but people saw Alice and duly reported to Mrs. Buxbaum. Out of fear her daughter might become a Catholic, Mrs. Buxbaum returned to school and demanded her daughter back.

From that point on, Alice and her mother engaged in constant struggle. Alice, reluctant to reveal her fervent desire to seek and know God, resisted her mother's questions and secretly continued to recite her daily *Hail Mary*, while her mother grew more distrustful. The rift between Alice and her mother eventually became definitive. Alice insisted on joining the Church, and her mother refused. One day Alice's mother challenged her in exasperation: "Choose between me and becoming a Catholic, but I tell you that if you become a Catholic, you will never see my face again!" Weeping bitterly and unable to look her mother in the eyes, Alice said: "I choose to be a Catholic." Shortly after, Mrs. Buxbaum left the city, but she waited in Mexico in hopes Alice would change her mind. Alice, too, hoped that her mother would relent, but then the time came for Mrs. Buxbaum's departure by train from San Luis Potosi for eventual passage to England. Hearing the whistle as the train left the station, Alice's heart sank, and she never saw her mother again! The Carmel of Buffalo sits near train tracks above Shoshone Park, and years later, Little Mother remarked that the sound of the train whistles always pierced her heart.[4]

Thankfully a fervent Catholic family adopted Alice, who was only thirteen years old when her mother abandoned her. She prepared a full year for her Baptism on the feast of St. Monica, May 4. Alice, wearing the purple gown of a catechumen, expressed her desire to join the Church. "Alice, what do you ask of the Church of God?" "Faith!" After

---

[4] The description of Mother Mary of St. John of the Cross and her youth in Mexico are taken from personal accounts and the book by her Carmelite Sisters titled: *One Hail Mary* (1971). A woman of tremendous humility and strength, it was hard for Little Mother to speak about these details because of the difficult memories. It should be clear, though, that Mother Mary of St. John of the Cross harbored no ill feelings toward her mother for the rest of her life.

16

her Baptism, Alice became known as "Maria Elisa." Four days later she received first Holy Communion. Alice became active in the Church immediately. Unlike the United States, where Catholics identify with a parish church, Mexican Catholics join confraternities, which are societies for lay people to be affiliated with the spirit and traditions of a particular Religious Order. Alice and her Godmother were active in many confraternities. For example, she joined the confraternity of the Holy Rosary, whose members pledged to say fifteen decades of the rosary one hour each month. Alice chose from two to three in the morning because in her words, "it is the only hour I am sure of." Alice rose many nights to pray and continued this practice well into her Carmelite years.

Now a fixture in the Church around San Luis Potosi, Alice also offered priceless help to her Godmother. Her adopted sister, Maria, explained in a letter to the Community the simple but beautiful life that Little Mother lived in Mexico with her Godmother:

> They lived almost a monastic life, for they spent their time working for the Confraternities, especially that in honor of Our Lady of Mount Carmel. They worked for the Holy Rosary, Catholic Mothers, the Propagation of the Faith, and that of the Sacred Heart. She (Elisa) was universally loved by rich and poor, whom she treated with much charity. Whenever she went to the market, she was showered with gifts of fruits, vegetables, flowers, etc. As she was very much interested in art, she was put under an art teacher and became a very good artist, as you well know. She spent much of her time in painting and also gave several classes. She lived this simple life until she left for the convent. Kindness and simplicity in her manners were her outstanding qualities, and she was always cheerful and happy wherever she might be.

Maria married and left home, but Alice remained with her widowed Godmother. This good woman suffered a horrible accident resulting in a broken hip when a robber, fleeing the police, ran her over. As a result,

Alice doubled her efforts around the house, while at the same time her devotion to the Confraternity of Our Blessed Lady of Mt. Carmel increased. Often while dressing a statue of Mary (a common custom in Mexico), Alice's desire to become a Carmelite overwhelmed her. Like Mother Elias, Alice faced the same revolutionary strife in Mexico, and she also had to bear a particular cross sent by the Lord Himself.

Alice baked a special meal for a priest friend of the family on his feast day. When she went to deliver the meal, Alice met a young girl on the street who asked for prayers for a family member stricken with smallpox. Alice fell ill that night. The doctor came and ordered everyone out of the home, including her invalid Godmother, as a precaution. Alice then endured a bitter fight with feverish bouts, which she compared to being dipped in an ice-cold lake. After days of struggle between life and death, she awoke surrounded by loved ones. God had spared her. While Alice had completely missed the feast of Our Lady of Mt. Carmel on July 16, the desire to be consecrated to Christ and His Mother as a Carmelite now consumed her.

Alice went to church and told the priest in the confessional about her call to Carmel. Because this was not Alice's regular confessor, he scolded her: "What ingratitude to think of leaving your Godmother who has done so much for you! What black ingratitude!" Mortified at this rebuke, she prayed for discernment over the next few weeks and came to understand that God's will might be for her to remain with her Godmother. But Alice went to the confessional and summoned the courage to mention her vocation yet again. As Providence would have it, she met the same priest as before. But this time he agreed that a vocation to Carmel was indeed God's will! The priest explained that in Alice's previous confession, he was merely testing her to determine the strength of her vocation. The priest told Alice that he knew a group of Carmelite nuns, recently exiled from Mexico, who were now living in Grand Rapids. He gave her the address of Mother Carmen, the new Prioress, and Mother Elias.

Over the next few months, Alice corresponded with Mother Carmen, all the while keeping this secret from her Godmother. She knew that her leaving for the United States and embracing a life in the cloister would certainly be difficult for her Godmother, even though her Godmother would still have her daughter to take care of her. So, she enlisted the help of a local priest to break the news. Despite Alice's good intentions, her Godmother bitterly scorned her, likely due to her failing health. Heartbroken, Alice still followed God's will for her to become a Carmelite, and so she began the long journey to the United States dressed in the secular habit of the Carmelite Order. Alice arrived in Grand Rapids on April 20, 1917. She was now forty-one years old.

From her first day in the monastery, she embraced her Carmelite vocation with wholehearted generosity. She also had the great grace of receiving as her Religious name Sister Mary of St. John of the Cross, her new patron saint being the great Spanish mystic and co-reformer of the Carmelite Order with St. Teresa of Avila. Mother Carmen soon recognized Sr. St. John's enormous gifts. Her steadfast commitment to learn the life and embrace its disciplines were evident from the start. In fact, Sr. St. John candidly told her amused Novice Mistress that she would seek to master obedience her first week in Carmel and then move on to humility. Her fervent desire to seek and know God, as well as her maturity, made adjustment to religious life relatively easy.

When the Carmel of Grand Rapids considered making a new foundation in Buffalo in 1920, the Prioress asked for volunteers to go. Non-committal, Sr. St. John told her superiors that she would do whatever God wanted. The Prioress and Mother Elias saw great potential in Sr. St. John, and so they selected her to be a part of the new foundation. After arriving in Buffalo, Mother Elias asked her to assume more and more responsibilities in the Community, and her confidence in Sr. St. John grew. Mother Elias eventually entrusted the new foundation in Buffalo to her leadership in August 1923 when leaving for Schenectady, obtaining the Bishop's permission for Sr. St. John to fulfill the remainder of her term as Prioress. Left alone with the young American Sisters, Little Mother quickly grew into her leadership role. Her strength, kindness, and holiness won not only the admiration of her Sisters, but also the local Buffalo community. Little Mother relearned the English language, forgotten due to the trauma of her mother having abandoned her, and turned an apparent obstacle into a strength. All who spoke with her were charmed by the quaint way she phrased things, including the occasional misstep, which she took with good humor. Just six years after she left Mexico to embark on her vocation, Mother Mary of St. John of the Cross now led the Carmel of Buffalo into a new and unknown future, trusting in the powerful protection of their spiritual sister in heaven, Therese of Lisieux.

***

The Cottage Street monastery sufficed for the time being, but it was not conducive to a rapidly growing foundation. On the outskirts of the city, however, sat the abandoned Rumsey estate, previously a hunting ground harboring old and rare trees. Bounded by Shoshone Drive, Carmel Road,[5] and Tacoma and Hertel Avenues, Fr. Crimmen buried a statue of the Little Flower on the property for good luck, and the land was soon deeded to the Discalced Carmelite Nuns of Buffalo thereafter. The Vatican announced that the beatification of the Little Flower would take place on April 29, 1923, the final step before her eventual canonization in 1925. When this news reached the Carmel of Buffalo, it prompted enthusiastic action. Mother Elias wrote to the Prioress of the Carmel of Lisieux, informing her of the plan to build a monastery in her name in Buffalo:

> When we began our foundation here, we had neither money nor friends, absolutely nothing but the mercy of God, coming as poor exiles from Mexico, not knowing even the language. The house we have is not very large, but God has blessed us in so miraculous a way, that now it is very plain He wants a suitable convent if it is to be dedicated to His Little Flower. Last year we were able to purchase about five acres of the most desirable land here in Buffalo, and hope, with the grace of God, to begin building our new convent about the middle of this year, and now we have decided to lay the cornerstone on the day of our Little Sister's beatification, April 29, 1923. We intend to build a fairly large convent and chapel, similar to our dear Carmel in Spain.

Mother Elias proceeded to ask for any relics that could be sent from Lisieux, because "there are about 50,000 people here in Buffalo who

---

[5] Fr. Crimmen convinced the landowners and the city that the street name should be "Carmel" because of its biblical significance for all religious denominations

are so devoted to the Little Flower." The Carmel of Buffalo celebrated its first public service in honor of the Little Flower on the day of her beatification with enormous crowds overflowing onto Cottage Street.

Although the Carmel of Buffalo now had land for a new monastery, it had reached its maximum debt and could not afford to build a new structure. Little Mother turned to Buffalo for help and established the Carmelite Building Fund. She widely disseminated the following appeal:

> Dear Friend:
>
> Please help save the health of these saintly Nuns who were persecuted by Villa and had to flee from Mexico. Because of their fidelity to Our Blessed Lord they have undergone a frightful and prolonged martyrdom. Their present crowded condition, after so many sufferings, is greatly endangering the health of these intrepid women. We ask you to assist these Nuns to build an absolutely necessary Convent. The cost of building necessitates this appeal.
>
> A perpetual Novena will be made by the Nuns of the Buffalo Carmel for all donors. God bless all who assist in this work of charity.

Buffalo responded, and Bishop Turner helped lay the cornerstone for the building on September 14, 1924, with 5,000 people in attendance. The Bishop also approved the Carmelites' plan to do something that perhaps had never been done before—dedicate a new chapel on the same day as the canonization of its patron saint. At the ceremony for the laying of the cornerstone, Father Eugene Regan poignantly preached of the "mustard seed" being planted in north Buffalo:

> The completion of this beautiful edifice will mark another step in a procession of the Roman Catholic faith—the faith of Jesus Christ. His teachings are as a mustard seed: when a handful is sown it grows and multiplies, until the time when it will reach all the peoples of the earth. We should be thankful that

the Lord has gifted us so that we may build beautiful structures as this in which to worship Him.

Let us hope that this new Carmelite convent, built in the name of the Blessed Therese of France, may be completed by the time of her canonization. It will mark a new epoch of Catholic devotion in the North Park Section.

The Little Flower's canonization was just eight months away, but Buffalo's winter would soon arrive. Work proceeded quickly, and Little Mother's enthusiasm pushed the workers along. Her industriousness and knowledge of the trades impressed the workers, and one commented: "Whatever work Mother plans can be accomplished." All the Sisters knew that God's grace and Therese's intercession would ensure the chapel's timely completion, and as 1925 arrived, all preparations were in place for the momentous event.

The Sisters packed all of their belongings on Cottage Street and came to the new monastery during a pouring rainstorm on April 19, 1925. By this time, "Little Lucy," Sister Lucy of the Blessed Trinity, was seriously ill and had to be transported by ambulance. Fr. Crimmen joined her in the ambulance, while carrying the Blessed Sacrament from Cottage Street to the new enclosure. With the bells ringing on Carmel Road for the first time, the nuns processed into the beautiful new chapel, as throngs of well-wishers and friends looked on. Only two years after the beatification of the Little Flower, and a mere seven months after laying the cornerstone, the new chapel was complete.

Bishop Turner joyfully greeted the nuns upon their arrival. He would soon leave for Rome to attend the canonization of the Little Flower. Fr. Bernard Fuller gave the sermon that day titled "Why This Waste?" In his remarks, he wondered whether those passing by during construction asked themselves why this large, beautiful chapel for a dozen poor nuns? Even worse, when society is faced with so many problems like illness, unemployment, and poverty, why do these nuns retreat to the cloister? In sum, why Carmel?

Fr. Fuller then answered those questions and explained that these lives, singularly devoted to God and prayer obtained His mercy and His

Grace for all our shortcomings. Prophetic words, which remain just as true almost one hundred years later:

> Is there a vocation more sublime, is there a purpose more divine? And is there anyone in God's Church who dare ask "Why this waste?"

> So farewell, Brides of Christ, as you go to bury yourselves in Christ. Mexico's loss was America's gain, and God bless the devoted Shepherd of our flock who, an exile himself, and who knows what it is to be far from home and native land for so paternally protecting your first exile community and so generously promoting this new home. You are the pride of our city, and this building raised through the offerings of devoted friends, shows how Buffalo appreciates the treasure that it has in you.

Benediction followed Fr. Fuller's remarks, and then Bishop Turner led the Sisters to the enclosure door. Ensconced now in their sacred cloister, lighted candles in hand, the Carmelites of Buffalo had a new home, one they would only trade for Heaven.

On the day of St. Therese of Lisieux's canonization in Rome, May 17, 1925, the chapel of the Carmel of Buffalo was officially dedicated to the Little Flower and became the Carmel of the Little Flower of Jesus. The Sisters had meticulously planned the timing of the ceremony so that, immediately after the Pope declared Little Therese as Saint Therese of the Child Jesus, the monastery would receive a telegram prompting them to commence the ceremony. Bishop Michael Fallon of London, Ontario, presided, and Carmel held three services that day to accommodate the tremendous crowds. Thus, the monastery had the first chapel in the world (so far as they know) dedicated to Saint Therese of the Child Jesus. The monastery's chronicles recorded this momentous event:

> Thus closed that longed-for day,
> When Little Therese and her Little Way
> Caused bells to chime from great
> Saint Peter's dome,

And pilgrim-throngs to gather into Rome;
While here in Buffalo was a sight unique,
For, scarcely would the Holy Father speak,
When she the Titular would be
Of her first church—across the wide, wide sea.

Standing before a Mexican firing squad, Mother Elias had asked Little Therese to rescue her if she was a saint. The Little Flower did save her, and now she was indeed a Saint!

***

Drawn by the presence of the new chapel, more people started to move into the neighborhood, creating the need for a parish church for Catholics in the area. The monastery seemed to some an ideal choice, but Little Mother thought otherwise. The Sisters could not live their cloistered life and at the same time accommodate the normal services that a parish offers like funerals and weddings. She presented these concerns to the Bishop, and he agreed. Instead of establishing a new parish at the monastery, Bishop Turner appointed Fr. Crimmen to be the first pastor of the new parish, St. Rose of Lima, in November 1925.

The Sisters also needed an outdoor space for fresh air and healthy recreation at the new monastery, without jeopardizing the privacy of the cloister. For this reason, the Carmelites soon began work on an enclosure wall. At first, the city did not agree to the height of the wall mandated by Carmelite tradition, but eventually the two sides negotiated a twelve-foot wall. At the same time, the monastery constructed a new wing for the Extern Sisters. Externs are not bound by the cloister and lived at that time in a separate area of the monastery. Both the Extern wing and the enclosure wall were completed on the same day in March 1927. The Sisters were happy because, for the first time, they could maintain the cloister and enjoy the outdoors.

The Carmel of the Little Flower of Jesus, as visitors see it today, was complete. At the corner of the property stands the large chapel, and the Extern wing extends along Tacoma Road toward Shoshone Park. The infirmary and cloister wing of the monastery sit along Carmel Road. Large white walls enclose the entire property. Approximately two to three acres in all, a large interior garden flourishes in the center. In her Constitutions, St. Teresa of Avila prescribed: "The walls should be as strong as possible; those of the enclosure high, within which there shall be ample ground so that the Religious may build some hermitages, to which they may retire for prayer after the example of our Holy Fathers." For their Holy Mother, the cloister garden provided a suitable place of prayer, and a place where the Sisters could contemplate the beauties of nature which lift the mind and heart to their Creator. But having experienced the Mexican Revolution and knowing the Sisters' need for exercise after five stifling years on Cottage Street, the Bishop and Little Mother were inclined to make the garden a place of intense manual labor.

When Bishop Turner came to visit the new additions, he gave Little Mother a gift of rose bushes to plant along the interior wall that received generous morning sun. He sent his gardener to cover this strip of ground with a fresh foot of the best topsoil and rose bushes. He also gave Mother a book on the cultivation of roses. The nuns were delighted. Mother asked Bishop: "But, what about the rest of the land, your Excellency?" The Bishop answered: "That is for you, Mother. Cultivate the ground. We want the Sisters to dig; don't let them just walk around in contemplation, but they should get forks, shovels and spades. The Sisters will not just get exercise, but also draw closer to God." Little Mother's ears perked up at the Bishop's answer, because she too planned all along to put her Sisters to work.

Little Mother led all the Sisters into the field to plant flowers for the altar and vegetables for the table. Unbeknownst to the Sisters, the ground sorely needed cultivation and help. Little Mother reported their work to the Prioress of another Carmel:

> When the fence was being erected, plans were made for us to have a beautiful park with rolling lawns, but I had said to myself: 'Not in my day.'
>
> So we set to work to prepare the ground for planting vegetables. We began to remove the stones, some of them were so large that it would take five or six Sisters to drag one on a burlap bag or an old broom, so as to roll it, thus bringing it as close as possible to the gate (not opening it, of course); so that would cost us less when it was time

to have them taken away. They took twelve of the largest truckloads of them.

Then we tried digging with forks and shovels but could do almost nothing on account of the hard clay. It was like stone in dry weather and like glue when it rained. It seemed hopeless to cultivate it.

We kept on clearing off the tin cans and broken bottles and stones, and then covered the entire garden with about a foot of ordinary fine sand, having been told that this was the only way to break up the clay. This was left on the ground, and after it was sinking we took forks or shovels and turned the ground, mixing the sand and clay. For several years we went through the same operation, adding sand and turning it into the ground—not very deep …

Now our ground is very loose and sandy, and one would think we never had anything but magnificent planting soil.

The work to clear and improve the soil continued for years, and the Sisters adapted to the strenuous manual labor. Not surprisingly, their health improved. Little Mother had been suffering from an ulcer for years, but soon she had relief. One day the local pharmacist called the monastery and asked Mother, "Have we offended you in some way?" Mother of course said no, and then the pharmacist said: "Mother, you and the Sisters no longer order any medicine from us." Little Mother laughed and told him about their energetic work in the garden.

Little Mother was very industrious and intelligent in the work. Always first to the garden, dressed in an apron, boots, and a wide-brimmed straw hat, she weeded and watered the plants tirelessly. One of her improvements was a watering system with pipes placed five inches beneath the ground, dividing the garden into squares. In each square, the Sisters put in the center a pipe three feet high that extended from the underground piping with a faucet. When turned on, it watered the entire square area. A plumber who helped Little Mother and the

Sisters with the project loved the idea and appreciated the nuns' ingenuity.

Improvements to the garden also developed through the efforts of friends. And there was no better friend to the monastery than Msgr. Nelson Baker. He wrote to Little Mother in November 1927 stating: "Kindly let us know whether you desire us to send you the manure now, or in the spring." He sent manure to Carmel until it covered the entire garden in fertilizer to about one foot in depth. The Sisters would load wheelbarrows with manure and continually work the soil. Finally, they planted seeds to reap the benefits of their hard work. Msgr. Baker noted: "Knowing that you will enjoy very much, seeing your little vegetable garden sprouting up nicely, and you will soon have all kinds of nice vegetables on your table, by your own production."

The correspondence between Little Mother and Msgr. Baker continued for many years, up until his death in July of 1936. Much of the correspondence reports on the fruits of the garden that Carmel would give. He was so proud of these gifts:

> I called all of my friends in, to witness the beautiful array of vegetables, being you might say, the first fruits of your garden, and I was very much envied by everyone, who did not have the chance to partake of so great a luxury as you gave us, and they all wondered how you could have developed so beautiful a crop in such a short time.

Msgr. Baker knew the answer:

> I told them it was done by, Yes! Sanctified hands and fingers which Our Lord was pleased to place over your beautiful garden … we know that when He blessed the garden, that things would grow to their fullest extent to my dear friends amongst your children, my sincere gratitude for their extraordinary efforts in making this little gift so attractive and edifying.

As the Vicar General of the Diocese, Msgr. Baker could enter the cloister, and he often did to witness the Sisters' hard work firsthand.

Although Little Mother loved to see the Sisters' zeal in manual labor, she never ignored the more important work of observance of the Rule and prayer. Little Mother also attended with solicitous care to the Sisters' dietary needs, which now included the wonderful blessing of fresh vegetables. In Carmel, the Sisters do not eat meat, and so vegetables are an important part of the diet. Little Mother placed great importance on the cook's role, and while she had at first emphasized simple preparations, she changed her mind as manual labor became a more significant part of the daily regimen. She frequently directed the Sisters to prepare nourishing and tasty dishes based on well-known Mexican recipes and would sometimes go to the kitchen herself to oversee the cooking. The Sisters would afterward comment with delight: "Our Mother has been in the kitchen!" Little Mother instilled in the Community the understanding that nourishing meals were essential for the Sisters, since this enabled them to pray with an alert and healthy mind.

Little Mother's impact in the early years of the Carmel of Buffalo was both profound and understated at the same time. Little in stature, she carried herself with tremendous humility. St. Therese had taught the Novices in Lisieux that God was "waiting for you in the fruitful valley of humility," and Little Mother indeed found God there. She continued to serve the Community in the office of Prioress and Subprioress throughout the 1930s and 1940s. She had two passions throughout all her years in Carmel: a boundless love for Jesus and Mary and also for the Order of Carmel.

Elected again as Prioress in 1945, Little Mother carried out her duties with the usual vigor, but her health steadily declined until her death on November 20, 1949. Almost thirty years after arriving in Buffalo, Little Mother went to her eternal Home. As the bells tolled and the casket rolled down the center aisle of the chapel on Thanksgiving Day 1949 (which coincided that year with the feast of St. John of the Cross), her daughters prepared to carry on life in Carmel without her. While this was a daunting challenge, Little Mother had taught her Sisters that perseverance in Faith, hope in God, and love for one another would triumph over all. Her lasting impact gave the Carmel of the Little Flower of Jesus a series of strong Prioresses, who strove to follow in her footsteps. With seedlings planted and strong roots established, the monastery flourished.

28

3

The Spirit of the Carmel of the
Little Flower of Jesus

"In the Heart of the Church My Mother, I will be love."

St. Therese of the Child Jesus

The term "charism" expresses the way a particular Order follows Christ—the identity, spirit, and grace that animates religious life. The Carmelite charism is to live in unceasing prayer hidden with Christ in God, in imitation of and in union with His Blessed Mother.

Although the Carmelites may be regarded as a "strict" Order, the Sisters' singular devotion to the love of God makes their life of self-sacrifice a joyful one. Pope Pius XII captured why the Carmelite pursues her vocation:

> This noisy and inconsistent century misunderstands and rejects a life lived apart, dedicated to contemplation, because it regards it as profitless activity, a detriment to the human society. You at least know well that no work is more capable of drawing down the Divine Benevolence and of aiding one's neighbor than this perpetual sacrifice of praise and the example of a life that is wholly pure.

The Carmelite's every action draws down grace from God for an increasingly grace-less world.

At the Carmel of Buffalo, St. Therese's Little Way characterizes in a particular manner how the charism is lived. Like their Patroness, the Sisters strive to do small things with great love, living always in the presence of their merciful Father, and seeking to please and console the Heart of Jesus. St. Therese approached sainthood as a child rather than through complicated theories, writing:

> Sometimes when I read books in which perfection is put before us with the goal obstructed by a thousand obstacles, my poor little head is quickly tired. I close the learned treatise which wearies my brain and dries up my heart, and I turn to the Sacred Scriptures ... Then all becomes clear and light ... I see that it is enough to acknowledge our nothingness and like children to surrender ourselves in the arms of God.

Unfortunately, because of her simplicity, St. Therese's Little Way can be misunderstood. But the Little Way merely restates what Jesus proclaimed in His Sermon on the Mount—"Blessed are the poor in spirit, for theirs is the kingdom of heaven." The spiritual childhood she envisioned was not childishness, but the humble acceptance of one's poverty and littleness before this great God whose paternal heart is always yearning to bestow his mercies upon us. In calling us to become children, she acknowledges before God, who is perfect, we must come with humility and trust. As St. Therese described, she was "a little soul who can offer only very little things to God." Although simple, her ordinary life knew no bounds when it came to her love for God. The Little Way—to do all things with great love—she described as a heart on fire:

> Charity gave me the key to my vocation. I saw that if the Church was a body made up of different members, the most essential and important one of all would not be lacking. I saw that the Church must have a heart, that this heart must be on fire with love. I saw that it was love alone which moved her other members, and that, were this love to fail, apostles would no longer spread the Gospel and martyrs would refuse to shed their blood. I saw that all vocations are summed up in love, and that love is all in all.

The Sisters of the Carmel of Buffalo seek to emulate the Little Flower's ideal to do all things with great love.

Having been passed down through the generations with its rich history, the spirit of the Community is palpable when one visits its

30

chapel. It is evident to all those with open hearts who come in contact with the monastery. Despite all the turmoil and change in the Church and society over the past hundred years, the Sisters have sought to remain faithful to St. Therese and her teachings, striving to imitate the heroic example of Mother Elias and Little Mother St. John.

Mother Elias and Little Mother ensured in the early years that the Sisters would have an ardent love for Jesus Christ, expressed in a generous following of St. Therese's Little Way. When Mother Elias officially resigned as Prioress on June 5, 1923, before going to Schenectady, she appointed Little Mother as the new Prioress. Despite this change in leadership, Little Mother humbly deferred to Mother Elias for the few remaining months of her time in Buffalo. Little Mother did so in a modest and unassuming way. This example was reminiscent of the early days of the Order, when the Holy Mother St. Teresa of Avila would appoint one of her Sisters to serve as Prioress of a new foundation, and the new Prioress would obey the Holy Mother during the time that she remained in that monastery.

Mother Elias made the most of her final months in Buffalo. She took each of her American Sisters aside for personal talks, reminding each nun that she would ultimately have to give account to God for the vocation entrusted to her. Mother Elias exacted promises from the Sisters to hold true to the Constitutions of their Holy Mother St. Teresa, even to the point of persecution or death. This exhortation came from a woman who had done just that: she had faced persecution and death, all the while remaining faithful to her vows. She also held up Little Mother as an example of how each Sister ought to give herself to the Order. Mother Elias gave each nun a different part of her Holy Habit, such as her Choir mantle, black veil, Scapular, and other articles. These were small gifts, something for the young Sisters to treasure and remind them of the sacred trust that Mother Elias had placed in their hands.

By the time Mother Elias left in August 1923, she had established a firm and conscientious discipline rooted in the Rule. When the bells rang for acts of Community, the Sisters answered eagerly as Mother Elias had taught them. Little Mother did not hesitate to change plans if she noticed a Sister's self-will taking precedence, or if she sensed a spiritual imperfection in the performance of daily tasks. It was not enough that work got done, if that work meant a departure from obedience or prayer. During recreation, Little Mother told stories about Mother Elias and the Mexican Sisters, in Schenectady and Grand Rapids, and reminded everyone of their promises. Little Mother implored the Sisters to be courageous in the face of adversity and to place their trust in God.

***

A unique way in which the Sisters have expressed their love for Jesus Christ over the years has been the production of handmade crucifixes, a work begun by Little Mother herself. The Mexican people, following the Spanish tradition, liked to depict the sufferings of Our Lord on painted crucifixes as a sign of devotion to Christ's Passion. Having taken lessons from a renowned professional as a child, Little Mother became a fine artist. The monastery had a life-sized crucifix, and Mother Elias asked Little Mother to try her hand at painting it to portray Christ's wounds more vividly. Bowing her head to the Prioress, she said: "I have never done any work like that Mother; I do not know how to go about it, but if you want me to try, I shall do so."

Little Mother slowly began to apply her skillful brush to the large crucifix, and with time it depicted the great tenderness of Christ's face and vivid details of the Lord's bodily wounds. Not long after its completion, visitors asked where this crucifix came from. After being told that one of the Sisters had done this work, people would sometimes ask if she could paint or repair crucifixes for them too. Little Mother obliged and continued this work the rest of her life. In doing so, she touched the local community by her labor and devotion, while remaining hidden in the heart of the Church.

It all started with her simple reply, "if you want me to try, I shall do so." In humble obedience, she found joy in following the Little Way. Truly, it was love alone that mattered.

Inspired by the infinite sacrifice of their Divine Spouse and the heroic example of St. Therese, the Sisters had the fortitude to face the departure of their beloved Mother Elias for Schenectady on August 13, 1923, a monumental day for the fledgling monastery. Mother Elias's bravery, along with her firm but loving hand as Prioress, made her departure a great loss for the Community. When the appointed time came, Mother Elias and Little Mother told their Sisters that all goodbyes would be said at recreation the night before, and that on the morning of August 13, there would be no tears. But, when Little Mother locked the enclosure door after Mother Elias and the other Sisters left, she wept bitterly. Facing the Sisters whom she must now lead, Little Mother could not seem to control her tears. Although she desperately wanted to be strong, her emotions were too much to bear.

Then, Sister Frances Teresa walked up, embraced her, and with heartfelt tenderness said: "Mother, we'll do all we can to help you!" The tears stopped, and Little Mother directed everyone: "To the laundry!" Indeed, it was laundry day, and work provided a pleasant distraction for their heavy hearts. Sr. Frances Teresa's simple act of kindness and love for Mother showed the Little Way in action. Her small act of charity helped the Community regain its strength after Mother Elias's departure. A tiny ripple can indeed create a great wave.

As if 1923 were not hard enough for the nuns, this year also brought the loss of Sister Mary of the Incarnation and of the Holy Face (Maria Guadalupe Apolinania) in March, and then Sister Soledad of the Blessed Sacrament (Petra Jacoba Medina) in June. Sr. Mary had entered the monastery in Queretaro in 1909 at the age of seventeen. She endured the trials with Mother Elias in Mexico, made the journey to Grand Rapids, and eventually became one of the nuns to form the new foundation in Buffalo. However, Sr. Mary suffered a severe attack of pneumonia in 1921 and never recovered. Her suffering was great during the next two years, but she faced this adversity peacefully and with full knowledge that one day the Lord would relieve her of the burden.

Similarly, Sr. Soledad came from Queretaro, entering the monastery in 1914 at the age of twenty-one. She transferred to Buffalo in November 1920, six months after the other nuns had arrived. She was then sick for a few years prior to her death in 1923. The heroic virtue of these two Sisters made a profound impression on the young Community. It was not lost on the Sisters that both Sr. Mary and Sr. Soledad would continue their great work from heaven. From the earliest days, the Sisters have striven to treat the sick with the utmost charity and compassion, in imitation of their Holy Mother St. Teresa and their patroness, St. Therese. What Carmel may lack in state-of-the-art medical facilities, it makes up for with the gentle hand of Jesus

Christ, as the Sisters take care of the infirm. Their charity and love become a part of Carmel, passed down from old to young.

Carmel's charism combines both the sacrifice of Calvary and the intimacy of Nazareth. As Calvary rises against the sky in Jesus's complete self-offering to the Father for our redemption and as Nazareth captures Christ's hidden life with His Mother, so do the Sisters live a similar life of fruitful, hidden self-sacrifice. Carmel stands as a living testament to the love of Jesus Christ—He is the reason the Sisters give up everything to pursue their vocations.

In the early years, the founding Mothers, the Mexican exiles, and the young American Sisters built a strong foundation upon which the whole structure would be fitted together in love. The enclosure walls veil the monastery from the outside world, a fitting symbol of the way God's action in each soul is hidden from the eyes of others. The growth of each soul's interior garden, tended with care by the Divine Spouse, is veiled in mystery in this life. But each of these gardens will be revealed in all its glorious beauty in heaven, for the glory of the Divine Gardener of souls.

The Carmel of Buffalo's Foundress:
Mother Mary Elias of the Blessed Sacrament

"Little Mother" with a Bounty of Flowers and Vegetables:
Mother Mary of St. John of the Cross

Laying of the Cornerstone and Construction: 1924-25

Canonization Day of St. Therese May 17, 1925

Working in the Garden

**Sr. Mary Agnes of Jesus
(Edna Bush)**

Community Procession 1940s

**Mother Veronica (ladder)
and Mother Mary
St. Joseph (holding bucket)**

**Sr. Teresa of Jesus
(Catherine Nash)**

II
THE INTERIOR GARDEN

4
The Vocation

My beloved is my Bridegroom. And my Lord—O what a joy!

St. John of the Cross

A vocation to Carmel begins a life-long love affair with the Lord. God touches a woman deep in her heart and the yearning for Him propels her forward. A woman answering the call to Carmel not only embarks on a new way of life, but also radically departs from the world—a heroic choice and a unique call from God.

The Carmelite Order attracts young women for a variety of reasons. First, Carmel's devotion to Mary, our Blessed Mother, provides a beautiful example of discerning and fulfilling God's will: "Behold, I am the handmaid of the Lord. May it be done to me according to your word." (Luke 1:38) Second, the traditional Carmelite life of prayer gives women an opportunity to live out a deeply religious life because Carmelites not only profess the Gospel in words, but also in their dedicated lives. Finally, the Carmelites inspire us to live our Faith lives with zeal and conviction. Indeed, the Carmel of Buffalo's history and its foundation by Mother Elias and Little Mother make others want to follow in their footsteps. The sacrifices that both of these women made to establish the Carmel of the Little Flower of Jesus make future Carmelites want to build on this tremendous legacy and tradition.

Over time, the call to Carmel has certainly changed. In St. Teresa of Avila's day (sixteenth century Spain), women often joined the monastery because of limited options, marriage being the only other vocation. By 1920, when the Carmel of Buffalo was founded, options for women had certainly improved, but still few careers were truly open. Suffragettes had just won women the right to vote in the United States. Today, on the other hand, women can pursue many different careers. Amidst the competing alternatives, it takes a unique woman touched by a special grace to discern a call to Carmel's radical life. Ultimately though, women come to Carmel because of a deep, spousal love for Christ. The adjective "spousal" might seem inapt to those unfamiliar with the spiritual life. But "spousal" love means that a woman encounters Jesus's presence deep in her heart and wants to sacrifice all other attractions to be with Him. She desires to give every fiber of her being to Him. An overwhelming conviction develops: "I have to be on the other side of that wall."

Women enter at all stages of life. The Carmel of Buffalo has welcomed a widow with children, Sr. Mary of the Incarnation (Mary Elizabeth Nash) who entered at age seventy-two and received the Habit from her son, Father John Nash, SJ, and Sr. Mary Grace of the Immaculate Heart of Mary (Margaret Veronica Doherty), who entered and left two times before joining for good in 1967. However, the typical age for entrance is between eighteen and thirty-five. An applicant to Carmel begins the process when she writes the Prioress of a particular monastery and is invited to come for a visit. The Carmel of Buffalo does not permit "trial runs" within the enclosure, but women can visit to meet the nuns and discuss a possible vocation. Although there are many Carmelite monasteries in the United States, a woman usually feels an affinity for a particular one. If the visits and meetings go well, the candidate fills out a written application, and the Community votes whether or not to accept her. If accepted, the woman makes the necessary preparations to leave the world and begin formation.

Generally, formation to become a fully professed Carmelite requires: one year of Aspirancy, one year of Postulancy, two years of Novitiate, and several years of temporary vows before Solemn Profession. Each woman progresses at her own pace, and the workload varies from person to person. At first, the newcomer simply observes. She may feel vulnerable because everything is foreign to her. Just learning the basic ceremonies, the daily schedule, the monastic way of doing things, and the history and heritage of the Carmelite Order can be daunting. The urge to return home arises naturally because she must adapt to this new way of life, having just separated herself from family and friends. But thankfully Carmel is a life of love. The Novice Mistress personally oversees the formation of each candidate with maternal care. Contrary to popular opinion, monastic life is not cold and austere. A true family spirit pervades the Community and sustains the candidate as she takes her first steps. If she willingly leaps into God's arms, she will be rewarded. Those with a true vocation not only accept this new life, but eagerly divest themselves of worldly ways. The enclosure becomes natural to one who genuinely seeks Christ.

Having completed Aspirancy and Postulancy, the new Sister officially begins her Novitiate with the reception of the Holy Habit of Our Lady of Mt. Carmel and her new Religious name. This event is a great celebration. The Prioress, who prays for enlightenment from the Holy Spirit so that the name bestowed upon the new Novice reflects the unique personal vocation to which God is calling her, chooses the name. At Mass on the new Novice's Clothing Day, the priest reads her name aloud to the congregation for the first time. The Postulant no longer carries her original name, and she proudly bears her Religious name as a tangible sign of acceptance into this new life. The Novitiate, a two-year period, now begins. Novices study the Carmelite Rule and Constitutions, as well as the teachings of the Holy Parents of the Order, St. Teresa of Avila and St. John of the Cross. Studying the great works of these Saints, such as *Book of Her Life*, *The Way of Perfection*, and *The Interior Castle* (St. Teresa) and *Ascent of Mt. Carmel* and *Spiritual Canticle* (St. John of the Cross) draws the Novice to a deeper appreciation for Carmel's heritage and charism.

The Novice makes her First Profession of temporary vows after the two-year Novitiate. Vows are free and deliberate promises made to God in which the Sister binds herself to observe the evangelical counsels of obedience, chastity, and poverty. After Temporary Profession, there are several years before Final Vows. Initially, the Sister remains under the Novice Mistress's guidance. Then, at a time determined by the Prioress and Novice Mistress, the Sister leaves the Novitiate and lives among the Solemnly Professed members of the Community. Solemn Profession is public and perpetual. The Carmelite receives the black veil, which signifies her complete renunciation of the world and her total dedication to Christ, her Bridegroom.

Carmelite life presents an intellectual and physical challenge of the first order. The Sisters estimate that one in ten Postulants make it to Solemn Vows. That statistic reflects the magnitude of the challenge and does not mean nine women failed. Rather, God calls each of us to follow different paths, and if women leave Carmel, it is because the Lord is calling them to do something else with their lives. Likewise, the Community would never force anyone to stay. Some personalities simply are not open to formation. The "good of the whole" is vitally important, and if a candidate does not belong or does not fit in, it disturbs the entire Community. Her presence in the monastery becomes a detriment not only to her own peace and growth, but also to others. As St. Teresa said: "in this house where there are no more than thirteen—nor must there be any more—all must be friends, all must be loved, all must be held dear, all must be helped." When one does not have the grace to live the life joyfully, it disturbs this delicate balance, and it is a blessing for the individual and for the Community for this person to return to the world.

***

Certain virtues are characteristic of the Carmelite way of life, and they greatly assist the Sisters in their vocations. Virtues are distinct from vows. While vows are promises to do or not do a specific thing, virtues guide the will toward God in an aspirational way. Virtues give meaning to the vows. For example, a Carmelite can exteriorly observe the vow of poverty, but if she is still attached to the goods of this world in her heart, then the external observance will not really bring her closer to God. St. Teresa strongly recommended to her daughters the practice of three particular virtues as essential for a life of deep prayer: detachment, fraternal charity, and humility.

Detachment is an unfamiliar term nowadays, but it means that someone must "let go" of all earthly things. This attitude is fundamental to the Carmelite vocation. Just as boot camp in the military strips away the "civilian way" of doing things, Carmelites undergo a similar transformation, albeit for a very different reason. Divided affection is incompatible with true union with God. As St. Teresa explained, "the happy result of detachment is inner freedom, freedom from worry about bodily comfort, honor and wealth." In St. Teresa's time, when nobility, esteem, and honor were a large part of a person's place in the world, she asked her Sisters to let go of such worldly considerations. The world has changed considerably since the 1500s, but the concept of leaving earthly things behind has not. The Carmelite physically detaches herself from family and the trappings of our world, but she also has to interiorly leave these things behind for the sake of a greater love. She knows that, in making this sacrifice, God will reward her family with greater blessings than her mere physical presence could ever bring.

Every woman who enters Carmel leaves her family. Some leave parents who support her call to Carmel, while unfortunately others do not. Regardless, separation from family is difficult but necessary. Family visits are limited once a young woman enters Carmel. The Carmelite makes that sacrifice freely (and so do the families, though perhaps not as freely). In addition, a Sister must also strive to divest her memory of earthly experiences that preceded her entrance; she forgets the past so that she may press ahead. Of course, all Carmelites still love their families, but they forego familial love to focus solely on the love of Jesus Christ. As their relationship with Him deepens, so do the graces and blessings which flow to their families and beyond.

The walls around the monastery provide physical symbols of detachment. The Prioress protects the Community from anything that would disturb its recollection. News and distractions bombard us daily. The monastery wisely removes such obstacles because they fundamentally conflict with the goal of drawing inward. The walls also create an environment where the Sisters can observe exterior customs that strengthen their focus on the interior life. For example, the young Sisters are taught to practice "custody of the eyes," curtailing the common desire to look around curiously. The Carmelites speak quietly, politely, and in a unique God-centered way. Even greetings are different at Carmel. When two Sisters meet, the younger Sister says: "Praised be Jesus Christ!" and the senior responds, "Now and Forever!" All these customs provide constant reminders to look within and focus on the Lord. Like peeling away layers of an onion, God slowly strips away earthly trappings—the Carmelite no longer walks in the ways of our world, so that she may be wholly dedicated to following the Lord.

Detachment reveals the monastic life in all its richness and authenticity. The earthly world recedes, while the supernatural world comes to the fore. Detachment allows the soul to reach new heights and explore new boundaries in the spiritual life. As St. John of the Cross said, "the bird cannot soar toward the sun if it is attached to the earth, even by the slightest of threads." Detachment is a lifelong process in which the Sister increasingly pulls away from the world to draw closer to the Creator. Carmelites speak of "dying to the world" because they are consumed with one desire alone: the anxious desire to possess Christ. The virtue of detachment has a "totality" difficult for lay people to understand. Absolute renunciation of worldly things and the world itself defies the imagination, particularly for those of us still struggling up the lower slopes of Mount Carmel. But to the Carmelite, its totality brings the freedom to pursue God as a singular quest.

Charity lies at the heart of Carmelite life. To a Carmelite, fraternal charity signifies God's love as encapsulated in the two greatest Commandments: "Thou shalt love the Lord thy God with thy whole heart, and with thy whole soul, and with thy whole mind. This is the greatest and first commandment. And the second is like this: Thou shalt love they neighbor as thyself." (Matthew 22, 37-40) That is why the Little Flower encouraged her Sisters to always act with greater love because "our Lord does not look so much at the greatness of our actions, nor even at their difficulty, but at the love with which we do them." Charity makes us more like God, and therefore draws us closer to the divine life. It is the simplest of all virtues—to love—and yet the most difficult. The Carmelites nevertheless pursue charity in every circumstance: at prayer, at work, and in every personal interaction. For this reason, the love that emanates from Carmel is like no other because it has a purity and simplicity from God Himself.

Finally, humility animates everything a Carmelite does. Faith cannot grow without humility. Humility battles pride, a powerful destructive force that undermines the other virtues. Essential for monastic life, humility is the same virtue that St. Benedict repeatedly stresses in his famous Rule. The Carmelites' Holy Mother, St. Teresa of Avila, wrote in the *Interior Castle* that humility first requires self-knowledge: "Self-knowledge is so important that, even if you were raised right up to the heavens, I should like you never to relax your cultivation of it; so long as we are on this earth, nothing matters more to us than humility." With humility, a Carmelite understands her total dependence on God, a realization which puts everything into perspective: a Sister readily accepts the Prioress's commands, desiring to obey because she knows it is God's will; labor, although physically tiring, becomes a sacrifice for the glory of God; and her joy increases the more she regards herself as the least and the servant of all.

Along with the observance of the vows and the virtues, the Carmelite vocation is characterized by a deep and profound devotion to Our Lady. An ancient motto states: "Carmel is all Mary's." The Prophet Elijah prayed on Mount Carmel for the salvation of Israel, which was suffering a drought. He saw a little cloud in the distant horizon and recognized it as God's answer to his hope-filled prayer. Elijah also understood that the cloud was a symbol of the Virgin who would one day bear the Savior. That purity of faith, hope, and love is what the Carmelite seeks as she ascends Mount Carmel. From their earliest days in the monastery, the Sisters are instilled with a profound love for the Queen of Carmel, whose Habit they wear.

In the end, each new vocation brings unique gifts to the Community, and the Carmelites perfect these gifts over a lifetime. New Sisters must regard their Superiors with a supernatural, childlike faith, confident that those whom God places over them will lead them surely on the path to Divine union. The Carmelite vows herself to God in heart and soul, with an unquenchable desire to find Him. This desire converges with the theological virtues of faith, hope, and charity given at Holy Baptism, and her unique gifts come to full fruition through this singular life of contemplative prayer.

***

The stories of Sister Mary Agnes of Jesus (Edna Bush) and Sister Teresa of Jesus (Catherine Nash) provide beautiful examples of the call to Carmel.

Edna Bush was born December 24, 1904, and she entered the monastery on September 8, 1925. Attracted to God at a young age, when Edna tired from playing she would say, "I have to rest and I am going to church to rest near Jesus." Similarly, while a student at Mount St. Joseph Academy, she had an intense love for St. Joseph, and she realized her vocation one day while gazing at St. Joseph's statue. Not a complicated call in any sense, Edna entered the cloister to pursue a love affair between God and her soul.

From her earliest days in Carmel, Sr. Agnes provided a shining example of obedience and humility. All Carmelites pursue these virtues, but Sr. Agnes did so with exceptional zeal. Her natural talents also seemed to know no bounds. She was gifted at sewing, drawing, and painting, not to mention gardening, carpentry, and masonry work—she did everything. Indeed, Sr. Agnes laid the concrete walkways in the cloister garden, with Little Mother overseeing her work. Because of her profound sense of obedience and her many gifts, Little Mother usually had Sr. Agnes at her side, a ready hand to help in

47

every task. But despite her obvious talents, humility marked every deed. Never wanting to "show off," Sr. Agnes did not hesitate to put aside her own work if any Sister requested help. On feast days, Sr. Agnes's hands would have touched almost all of the gifts prepared to mark the day. God gave her all these incredible talents, but she kept nothing for herself. She offered all for the greater glory of God. As a true Carmelite, humble of heart, Sr. Agnes would have been the last one to bring attention to her contributions to the Community. But the other Sisters did recognize her gifts and were profoundly impressed by her self-effacement and generosity.

Sr. Agnes possessed the simplicity of a child, but also the maturity of an older nun filled with God's grace. When she died on June 28, 1947, her Sisters marveled at her hands and feet ever active in life, now so quiet in death. Those same hands and feet had done so much for the Community over her twenty-one years of Carmelite life. Even though she died at the age of forty-two, half her life spent in the world and half in Carmel, Sr. Agnes's impact can be felt at the Carmel of Buffalo today. From generation to generation, her name often comes up—the "perfect Carmelite," always obedient and filled with humility. She is still someone whom the Sisters today try to emulate.

Sr. Teresa of Jesus, a contemporary of Sr. Agnes, provides another example of a beautiful vocation to Carmel. Born Catherine Mary Nash, she and her family made an indelible mark on the Carmel of Buffalo.

Sr. Teresa's mother, Lily Power, wanted to be a Carmelite at a young age. But at the turn of the century, when Lily was growing up, only a few Carmelite monasteries existed in America. A child prodigy in piano and voice, when Lily reached young adulthood, she attracted many suitors. She eventually married a young doctor named James Nash. Catherine, the second of Lily's nine children, was a frail child who tragically came close to death. Although foul play could not be proven, a stranger gave candy one day to Catherine and her sister Margaret Mary, the third child. The two girls fell deathly ill right after. Apparently poisoned, Catherine somehow battled through the illness, but her more robust sister died despite Dr. Nash's best efforts. Catherine's parents would never be the same, and they became even more devoted to young Catherine.

Catherine was a bright child, and her devout Catholic family members on both her father's and mother's sides influenced her upbringing considerably. Dr. Nash's brother, John, became a diocesan priest in Buffalo and a prominent figure in the local church. Lily Nash, her mother, always kept her affinity for the Carmelites, but it was Lily's sister Margaret who entered the new Carmelite monastery on Cottage Street, later becoming Mother Frances Teresa. Catherine's aunt and cousin were also Sisters at the monastery. Sensing a call to religious life herself, Catherine wrote to the Maryknoll Sisters her senior year of high school, but she never got a reply. The Carmel of Buffalo always ascribed this to Divine Providence. Then one winter day, Catherine visited the monastery. The Sisters' great charity made a profound impression on her, and she knew this was her call.

Although Catherine's family generally supported her vocation, Dr. Nash and his brother, the Monsignor, had reservations. Still in its infancy, the new monastery was not well established, and the Sisters were quite poor. Dr. Nash also knew that both Sr. Mary of the Incarnation and Sr. Soledad suffered from tuberculosis, and he worried that Catherine's frailty made her prone to sickness. Nonetheless, Catherine and her mother made a plan to get around Dr. Nash's objections. In the summer of 1923, while Mother Elias was planning to leave for Schenectady, Catherine attended Mass at the monastery on August 6, the Feast of the Transfiguration, all preparations had been made for her to enter the enclosure after Mass. Mother Elias planned on taking Catherine on the new foundation. Fearing Dr. Nash might learn of the plan, the Sisters locked the chapel door after Mass started. During the homily, a loud bang came on the door, and the nuns quickly ushered Catherine inside the cloister. The knocking continued, and much to the Sisters' surprise, it wasn't Dr. Nash after all.

Bishop Turner had come to visit, and when he heard of the circumstances, he agreed that Catherine should be a Carmelite, but not in Schenectady. Instead, Catherine would remain part of the Carmel of Buffalo and become Sr. Teresa of Jesus. Days and weeks passed. When it came time for Sr. Teresa to receive the Holy Habit, the custom at that time required that the Novice return briefly to see her family. Sister arrived home to find all waiting, except her father, who had shut himself upstairs. Sr. Teresa ran up and gave her father a big hug, which broke through his remaining resistance. Never angry with her, Dr. Nash only wanted what was best for his daughter, and he saw clearly how happy his Catherine would be in Carmel.

Sr. Teresa entered the monastery with a maturity and knowledge beyond her years. She soon quoted from the Carmelite's Holy Mother, St. Teresa of Avila, and knew exactly where to find important passages in her works. Not aspiring to be a Superior or Foundress, Sister strove to practice humility, obedience, and charity in all her works. She felt very blessed to have as her patronesses the saints, who in 1970, were to be declared the first two women Doctors of the Church: St. Catherine of Siena and St. Teresa of Avila. Her passion became the Order of Carmel, its history, and the life as professed in the Carmel of Buffalo. A gifted singer and organist, she taught other Sisters music and assisted the Community in learning Gregorian Chant. She generously served in the kitchen, laundry, sacristy, and garden. Eventually, Sister was elected to the Council, served as Subprioress, and became an invaluable source of advice for three Prioresses.

The Nash family produced abundant vocations. Sr. Teresa's sister Mary joined her at Carmel and became Sister Mary Elias of the Sacred Heart. Sr. Teresa's other sister Anne entered the Mercy Sisters and devoted herself to foreign missions. Her brother John became a Jesuit, served in World War II, and then worked in missions in the Caroline Islands. After Dr. Nash's death, Sr. Teresa's mother, who had remained devoted to Carmel as the organist at public services for many years, joined the Community as an Extern Sister, Sr. Mary of the Incarnation. Although we might conclude that having her own family at Carmel made Sr. Teresa's religious life easier, that was not the case. Since all members of the Community must be loved as Sisters, particular members must not be favored, even if they are family. Sr. Teresa, having an aunt (Mother Frances Teresa), cousin (Sr. Immaculata), sister (Sr. Mary Elias), and now mother (Sr. Mary of the Incarnation) in the same monastery, therefore, had to show restraint. Indeed, Sr. Teresa never told anyone about her thoughts and emotions surrounding the day her mother joined the monastery, and Sr. Teresa endured the sorrow of witnessing all those loved ones die before her.

Like Sr. Mary Agnes, Sr. Teresa also practiced great humility. She recognized that her talents must be submitted to obedience in love. Writing to a contemporary in the Carmel of Albuquerque who had

50

asked for advice on being the organist, she stated: "One must be tried and seared by humiliations and exercises in detachment, as an athlete must be prepared for the steep ascent or maneuver he is to face during his whole life.... Here no one may abide unless he is ready to humble himself with his whole heart for the love of God and take the last place." Sr. Teresa died on April 26, 1985. Bishop Edward Head presided at her funeral, and her brother Fr. John Nash assisted. As the Queen of Carmel enveloped Sr. Teresa beneath her mantle, peace settled over the Community, as if she were saying to the Sisters: "To you I leave my spirit of joy and humility."

St. John of the Cross described the Carmelite vocation as a love story between God and the soul:

To
CHRIST JESUS, THE BELOVED
My beloved is my Bridegroom
And my Lord—O what a joy!
I will henceforth all the powers
Of my soul for Him employ;
And the flock that once I tended,
Now I tend not as before
For my only occupation
Is to love Him more and more.

I have gone away forever
From the haunts of idle men
And a sharer in their follies
I will never be again.
They may say, and say it loudly,
I am lost; but I am not;
I was found by my Beloved,
O how blessed is my lot!

Though no formula exists of what it takes to be a Carmelite, a Discalced Carmelite saint, St. Maravillas of Jesus, counseled her Sisters: "On the outside be like everyone else; on the inside, be like no one else." All embrace the externals of the life for the good of the Community. But every Sister walks her own unique spiritual path. When each Sister embraces her call, it yields deep peace and joy after years of dedication and devotion. The seed, planted and nurtured in initial formation, blossoms into a lifetime of prayer, sacrifice, and work for the salvation of souls.

5

The Contemplative Life

Without prayer there is no Carmel.

Pope Leo XIII

Pope Leo XIII captured Carmel in these few words.

Prayer consumes the Carmelites because it is the door through which they enter the interior world of the soul, as the soul ascends toward God in prayer. Carmelites are professional prayers, and they need to be because their prayers advance the good of the Church. St. Teresa's teachings reminded her Sisters of that: "If your prayers and desires and disciplines and fasts are not performed for the intentions I have mentioned (in favor of the Church and Sacred Hierarchy), reflect that you are not carrying out the work, or fulfilling the object for which the Lord brought you here together."

Keeping vigil and standing guard, St. Albert of Jerusalem prescribed in the Carmelite Rule: "Each one shall remain in his cell or near it, meditating day and night on the law of the Lord, and watching in prayer, unless otherwise justly employed." The Sisters live out this oft cited part of the Carmelite Rule every day, and they see the monastery as a fortress to engage in spiritual warfare. St. Teresa of Avila described in *The Way of Perfection*:

> To return to the main reason the Lord brought us together in this house and why I have greatly desired that we live so as to please His Majesty, I want to speak of helping to remedy the great evils I have seen. Human forces are not sufficient to stop the spread of this fire caused by these heretics, even though people have tried to see if with the force of arms they could remedy all the evil that is making such progress. It has seemed to me that what is necessary is a different approach, the approach of a lord when in time of war his land is overrun with enemies and he finds himself

53

restricted on all sides. He withdraws to a city that he has well-fortified and from there sometimes strikes his foe. Those who are in the city, being picked men, are such that they can do more by themselves than many cowardly soldiers can. And often victory is won this way. At least, even though victory is not won, these chosen people are not conquered. For since they have no traitor, they cannot be conquered—unless through starvation. In this example the starvation cannot be such as to force them to surrender—to die, yes; but not to surrender.

Although St. Teresa's martial analogy may seem odd in modern times, the Sisters fervently embrace the idea. The Carmelites wear the Holy Habit of Mary, thought by some to resemble a knight's attire, and they understand what St. Teresa wanted her Sisters to become through vigilant prayer: "We [the Sisters] are the foundation stones of the Carmel of today and tomorrow. Let each one become such a stone that the building will stand firm forever." Scripture and their Holy Rule affirm that: "The life of man upon earth is a warfare." The Sisters will never betray their King, Jesus Christ.

Everything at the Carmel of Buffalo promotes this contemplative life of prayer, starting with enclosure. We view the large, white walls that surround the monastery as keeping the Sisters "in," but the Sisters know the walls "keep out" worldly distractions. The enclosure does more than just separate the Sisters from our noisy world. It also signifies a profound withdrawal from our world, which is spiritually necessary to fulfill the Carmelite vocation. The walls provide space for spiritual growth—an oasis where God can more easily be found within.

Even within the monastery walls, the Sisters embrace physical separation as a means to pursue spiritual growth. Each Carmelite has a separate cell that no one else may enter. The Rule's emphasis on a Carmelite "watching in prayer" *in* her cell is intentional because the cell provides a simple, austere place to meet the Lord. The bare cross on the wall, without an image of Christ, reminds her that, in embracing this life, she chooses to be crucified with Him. After a day of generous self-sacrifice, her body takes its rest there. More importantly, her spirit finds refreshment in the presence of God. Joyous in solitude and freed from distractions, she focuses her attention and affection on the Divine Guest dwelling within.

The Divine Indwelling, the doctrine that the Three Persons of the Blessed Trinity dwell in a soul in the state of grace, beckons the Carmelite to search for God within. St. John of the Cross described this inward journey in the Spiritual Canticle:

> What more do you want, O soul! And what else do you search for outside, when within yourself you possess your riches, delights, satisfactions, fullness and kingdom – your Beloved whom you desire and seek? Be joyful and gladdened in your interior recollection with Him, for you have Him so close to you. Desire Him there, adore Him there. Do not go in pursuit of Him outside yourself. You will only become distracted and wearied thereby, and you shall not find Him, or enjoy Him more securely, or sooner, or more intimately than by seeking Him within you.

This doctrine of the Divine Indwelling is popularly associated with the life and writings of another French Carmelite nun, who entered the Carmel of Dijon shortly after St. Therese died in Lisieux. St. Elizabeth of the Trinity (1880-1906) wrote: "If He did not fill our cells and cloisters, how empty they would be. But we see Him through everything, for we bear Him within us and our life is an anticipated Heaven." Thus, when the Sisters pray in their cells, keeping watch, He is never far away.

Along with the monastery's physical structure, a fixed daily schedule is of immense value for the contemplative life. Carmel's horarium structures the day around prayer. Here is the typical day:

> **5:15 a.m.** – The appointed Sister sounds the clappers, breaking the solemn silence with: "Praised be Jesus Christ and the Virgin Mary His Mother. Come to prayer, Sisters! Come to praise the Lord!" Each Sister echoes this prayer as she wakes from sleep.

5:45 a.m. – Rosary

6:00 a.m. – Lauds (Morning Prayer) is one of the seven Hours of the Divine Office (Liturgy of the Hours). At the end of Lauds, a bell is rung which marks the end of the Great Silence. The Sisters begin their morning meditation, communing with Our Lord in silent personal prayer for one hour.

7:15 a.m. – Terce (mid-morning prayer), another Hour of the Divine Office.

7:30 a.m. – Mass is the high point of the day for each Sister, as she clothes herself in a white mantle to remind her of that inner purity of soul which she should always possess. After Mass the Sisters partake of a small breakfast of bread and coffee, with some fruit in the summer.

9:00 a.m. – Manual labor: each Sister goes to her assigned duty – cooking, cleaning, sewing, gardening, and various other tasks, during which she works in solitude and silence as much as possible. Larger projects which are done as a Community (such as canning fruits and vegetables, washing and mending clothes, and "spring cleanings") are done in a spirit of silence and recollection.

11:00 a.m. – Sext (mid-day prayer), which is followed by the Litany of Our Lady. This time of prayer concludes with a five-minute particular examination of conscience, a spiritual exercise in which one focuses on a specific area of growth needed in the spiritual life. The Sisters then process to the Refectory (dining room) while reciting Psalm 129.

11:30 a.m. – Dinner: main meal of the day, taken in silence while listening to a spiritual book or conference. On special feast days the reading is omitted, so that the Sisters may take their recreation during the meal.

12:30 p.m. – Recreation: after dinner and dishes, there is a time of relaxation from the strict silence of the Rule, during which the Sisters converse in a spirit of joy and charity. At recreation they also do some sort of work, such as sewing, artwork, and gardening, except on Sundays and feast days.

1:30 p.m. – Free time.

2:00 p.m. – Each Sister retires to her cell for spiritual reading or quiet personal prayer.

2:55 p.m. – Chaplet of Mercy, followed by the Hour of None (mid-afternoon prayer).

3:15 p.m. – Manual labor.

4:55 p.m. – Evening meditation: as in the morning, the Sisters engage in silent personal prayer.

6:00 p.m. – Vespers (evening prayer).

6:15 p.m. – Supper: Carmelites fast from September 14 (the Feast of the Holy Cross) to Easter Sunday. During this time, supper is replaced by a light collation (a simple meal with divided portions). The Sisters observe continual abstinence from meat, except in case of sickness or infirmity, as the Rule prescribes.

7:00 p.m. – Evening recreation: same as the hour of recreation after dinner.

8:00 p.m. – Compline (night prayer), at the end of which the bell rings to announce the beginning of the Great Silence. The Sisters retire to their cells to pray, read, or work quietly.

9:00 p.m. – Matins (Office of Readings): this is the first Hour of the Divine Office for the following day.

10:30 p.m. – Retire for sleep, taking rest in the Sacred Heart of Jesus.

The daily schedule may seem repetitive and strict, but the Carmelites of Buffalo willfully follow this regimen, day after day, in a spirit of joyful sacrifice. And the Sisters never tire because it strengthens and fortifies the soul. Even though vocal prayer (the Divine Office) and Mental Prayer form only part of the daily schedule, the Sisters spiritualize every endeavor. Because love for God inspires their work, labor becomes a form of prayer. Similarly, because the Sisters encounter Christ in each other during Recreation, that too becomes a form of prayer. As a result, a Carmelite spends each day, in its entirety, in prayer and fully devoted to the One she loves.

Monotony is never a problem at the Carmel of Buffalo. Unlike the familiar lament, "If only I could find the right balance," Carmelites do not lack for balance because the daily schedule provides a blend of silent and vocal prayer, work, recreation, and meals. Indeed, the Carmelites find days that deviate from the regular schedule more challenging. Also, many feast days in the liturgical calendar and celebrations (anniversaries and birthdays) allow for special schedules and ample variety. In sum, the routine provides a rhythm and cadence so that Carmelites live keenly aware of His presence.

Finally, the solitude observed in Carmel promotes this contemplative life of prayer. The father of the Carmelites, the prophet Elias, said on Mount Horeb that, "God is not heard in the earthquake … but in the gentle whisper of the wind." (cf. 1 Kings 19.12) We tend to equate silence with being quiet or not talking. That is certainly a component of the Rule, which directs: "You should carefully avoid talking too much. For … in the multitude of words, there shall not want sin." But silence means more than just refraining from words. Silence constitutes the very atmosphere Carmelites live and breathe, enabling her to encounter God dwelling within. Silence pertains not only to exterior things (silence of the tongue, silence in one's movements), but also to the interior faculties (silence of the imagination, silence of the memory, silence of the desires of one's heart, if they crave anything but God). St. Elizabeth of the Trinity wrote:

On the mountain of Carmel, in silence, in solitude, in prayer that never ends, for it continues through everything, the Carmelite already lives as if in Heaven: 'by God alone'. The same One who will one day be her beatitude and will fully satisfy her in glory is already giving Himself to her. He never leaves her, He dwells within her soul; more than that, the two of them are *but one*. So she hungers for silence that she may always listen, penetrate ever deeper into His Infinite Being. She is identified with Him whom she loves, she finds Him everywhere; she sees Him shining through all things! Is this not Heaven on earth!

A constant dialogue between God and the Sisters continues each day, for the most part in silence. St. John of the Cross described this discourse in his *Maxims on Love*: "The language God best hears is silent love."

While the entire atmosphere at the Carmel of Buffalo promotes this contemplative life and helps the Sisters fulfill their vocations, it is the Sisters' resolute determination to find Christ in prayer that sustains the monastery. The Carmel of Buffalo exists for prayer, and this prayer has been the bedrock of its existence the last one hundred years. Unlike our attempts to pray a few minutes a day, while at Sunday Mass, and most likely in times of need, the Carmelites of Buffalo pray unceasingly. As St. Teresa instructed in *The Way of Perfection*:

> *Our primitive Rule states that we must pray without ceasing.* If we do this with all the care possible—for unceasing prayer is the most important aspect of the Rule—the fasts, the disciplines, and the silence the Order commands will not be wanting. For you already know that if prayer is to be genuine, it must be helped by these other things; prayer and comfortable living are incompatible.

Not for timid souls, the prayer life of a Carmelite entails hard work and sacrifice. Prayer has many degrees, like a waterfall, and each Carmelite experiences ups and downs. While the soul can sometimes experience consolation, the Sister can also experience difficult and arid periods and even feelings of despair and abandonment. To make these journeys, as St. Teresa described: "They must have a great and very resolute determination to persevere until reaching the end, come what may, happen what may, whatever work is involved, whatever criticism arises, whether they arrive or whether they die on the road, or even if they don't have the courage for the trials that are met, or if the whole world collapses." The soul anticipates with hope the graces that come with years of perseverance and receives from God sufficient grace to finish the journey. Carmelites remain committed to prayer because, like their Holy Mother, they are convinced that all goodness, all truth, all beauty, is to be found in Him. The Carmelite seeks the "one thing necessary," Jesus Christ, and in seeking Him they will find Him.

***

Hidden behind the walls, these stories are known to God alone. But if we cannot hear about these inward journeys, how can we recognize the beauty in these lives? The answer is perhaps summed up best by St. Elizabeth of the Trinity: "A Carmelite is a soul who has gazed on the Crucified, who has seen Him offering Himself to His Father as a Victim for souls, and recollecting herself in this great vision of the charity of Christ, has understood the passionate love of His soul, and has wanted to give herself as He did."

Prayer, sacrifice, and literally to give of themselves as He did are what make the Carmelite's life so beautiful. The Carmel of the Little Flower of Jesus is a hidden apostolate, meaning the monastery offers its prayer for the Church, the Mystical Body of Christ, and ultimately all of us, while hidden from the world. The monastery keeps it that way first and foremost so that it can actually accomplish the mission. But the consequence of that should not be we fail to see its beauty. Perhaps the easiest way to think about Carmel and see the beauty of this life is to think about selfless acts of love. Of course, the ultimate act of selfless love was Christ dying on the cross for all our sins. We are also familiar with selfless acts of love in our families and in the world around us. The Carmelite's life is one selfless act of love.

Love for Him and for us. A Carmelite loves God and seeks to magnify and reflect His love back to us. As the Gospel of John says: "My dear friends, let us love one another, for love comes from God.

60

Everyone who loves is born of God and knows God. Those who do not love, have not known God, for God is love." (1 John 4:7) Although hidden from us, the Carmelites' love colors and illuminates our mundane world. St. Therese, the Little Flower, aptly described how love changed her outlook of Our Lord's Living Garden:

> I understood that every flower created by Him is beautiful, that the brilliance of the rose and the whiteness of the lily do not lessen the perfume of the violet or the sweet simplicity of the daisy. I understood that if all the lowly flowers wished to be roses, nature would no longer be enamored with lovely hues. And so, it is in the world of souls, Our Lord's living garden.

Those Sisters at the Carmel of Buffalo make the Lord's living garden bloom—their love comes in prayer, in song, and also in the silence of their hidden apostolate.

The Carmelites of Buffalo speak to us each day and do not have to live in our world in order to speak to our world. We should listen because, more than anything, they desperately want to bring Christ to us and make us know His Love. They experience the burning thirst He has for souls and want to slake that thirst by bringing our hungry, wounded hearts to Him. Their sacrifices are offered with pure joy, to make their Divine Spouse better known and loved, and to enlighten the darkness of our wayward world with the radiance of His mercy. Those who have reached out and touched the monastery over the years can attest to the Sisters' ability to manifest Christ's love. Indeed, some might say that stories of the Carmel of Buffalo reaching beyond those white, cloister walls border on the miraculous. Whether miraculous or not, the Sisters do change lives and achieve wondrous deeds through prayer. Ronald Reagan once said: "Some people go through their whole lives wondering if they have made a difference. Marines don't have that problem." The same can be said about the Carmelites of Buffalo. They are a shining example of God's love here on Earth!

6
Keeping Watch in Prayer

Come and hear, all ye that fear God, and I will declare what he hath done for my soul.

Psalm 66

The monastery successfully weathered the early years of the 1920s and 1930s. Building on the foundation stones of humbled, exiled Mexican Sisters, the monastery not only survived but thrived under Little Mother's leadership, the generosity of the local Buffalo community, and God's grace. While vocations were abundant, the Great Depression and World War II brought tragedy and human misery to the world on a grand scale. The Carmel of Buffalo did its part to support the local community in this time of need, as well as pray for the servicemen overseas.

Sirens sounded on the morning of May 8, 1945, and a Catholic neighbor telephoned the monastery to tell them there was peace in Europe. A new day had dawned; the long war was over. The Sisters rang the tower bells, pealing them for over an hour in celebration. In 1945 the monastery also celebrated its Silver Jubilee (1920-1945) with a Pontifical Mass (a Solemn or High Mass celebrated by the Bishop using prescribed ceremonies) on the feast of the Little Flower, October 3. Little Mother asked the new Bishop, John F. O'Hara, to preside. Twenty-five years in Buffalo, and twenty years on Carmel Road, the monastery was now a permanent fixture.

While Carmel became an integral part of this north Buffalo neighborhood, it remained shrouded in mystery. Most of Buffalo likely wondered what the Carmelites did all day, and for the most part casual indifference marked its neighbors' general attitude toward the monastery: "they don't bother us, and we won't bother them." Although the public's attitude is understandable, the Sisters do not share our indifference. The Carmelites remain hidden, but they passionately care about the world and desperately want to reach us with their prayers.

The monastery's history includes many personal stories that demonstrate their power to invoke God's grace and reach beyond the cloister walls. Known only to the Sisters and those benefitted, which is how the Sisters prefer it, no detailed record exists of both mundane and miraculous events. The Sisters firmly believe in spiritual warfare—the classic struggle of good versus evil. The Sisters pray to God that we may find Him in our lives, and they are just fine not touting their successes. Seeing God shed His grace is reward enough for the Sisters, and despite the growing problems in our world, the Carmelites remain happy warriors.

The beautiful shrine (shown on the front cover) that now is the focal point of the monastery's interior garden provides just one example of God's intervention on the Carmelites' behalf in response to their prayers. Little Mother had always expressed the hope that one day the cloister garden would have a life-sized statue of Our Blessed Lady of Mount Carmel. The statue of Mary the Sisters already had was deteriorating badly. In the last month of Little Mother's life, November 1949, Isidore Jacoel wrote the monastery and said that he wanted to do something special for Christmas because he received a "very great favor" after the Sisters prayed for him. Little Mother wrote back and asked for a statue of Our Lady of Mount Carmel. Three days before Little Mother's death, she received his reply: "Our good St. Teresa will bring you the most beautiful statue of our Blessed Mother." Mr. Jacoel's generosity and fervor to help the Carmelites only increased after Little Mother's death. In his condolence letter, he wrote:

> I join the Community in grief in the passing of her Reverence Mother St. John of the Cross. She was a medium between God and me; she was also the conveyor of God's love to people everywhere. Humanity loses a saintly, loving and humble heart. I am confident that the Catholic Church will in due time have her Reverence canonized.

Little Mother was indeed an inspiration to many, but in Mr. Jacoel's case this relationship was all the more remarkable—he was Jewish.

Plans progressed and the monastery contracted with the Daprato Company to carve the statue and base. Bishop O'Hara arranged for

Mortimer J. Murphy to serve as the architect for the project. Mr. Murphy donated his services free of charge, and also designed a beautiful glass enclosure to encase the statue and protect it from the elements. When the Daprato Company requested payment in the fall of 1950, telling Mr. Jacoel that it would take at least nine months to complete, he generously paid in full and wrote: "delivery required by July 16, 1951." Quite providentially, this date marked the 700th anniversary of the bestowal of Our Lady's gift of the Brown Scapular. This Scapular, a miraculous gift with great power, has interesting origins. In the year 1251, St. Simon Stock, the General of the Carmelite Order, begged Our Lady to save the Order from persecution. Mary appeared to him on July 16, handing him the Brown Scapular. Her words were: "He who dies clothed with this habit shall be preserved from eternal fire." Pope Pius XII in 1951 had told the Carmelite Order that "he most willingly commended their decision to take all pains to pay homage to the Blessed Virgin Mary in as solemn a manner as possible on the occasion of the Seventh Centenary of the Institution of the Scapular of our Lady of Mount Carmel." The Carmel of Buffalo intended to do so with great enthusiasm.

Hopes were high after the Daprato Company responded that it would do everything in its power to deliver the statue by July 16. Bishop O'Hara agreed to celebrate a Pontifical Mass on that date, when the Carmel of Buffalo would erect and dedicate its statue of Mary. St. Therese, the Little Flower, also took an interest in the project, when the Daprato Company confirmed by letter on May 17 (the anniversary of the Little Flower's canonization) that the statue would ship from the studio in Italy on the SS. President Arthur to arrive in New York City on June 15. On June 27, the statue made it to the Carmel of Buffalo. The long wait was over! The Sisters peered through the wooden boxes holding the statue and its base. White marble radiated through. Steel scaffolding, riggers, and cables were constructed just to place the base and statue in place, which took another few days. Appropriately, on the Feast of the Visitation of Mary, July 2 on the traditional calendar, the Sisters' prayers were answered when the workmen unveiled the statue.

After hours of hard work to cement the image to the base, the statue was complete. It was ten minutes to noon, and Mother Rose of the Immaculate Heart of Mercy gathered all of the nuns. The sun shone out of a blue Buffalo sky, as if Little Mother was overseeing the work. The

Sisters never could have imagined so perfect a shrine to the Blessed Mother! The Infant smiling with His little arms extended seemed to say to the Carmelites of Buffalo, "Here We are for you!" The workmen shared the Sisters' joy and their appreciation for the statue's beauty. At evening recreation, the Sisters celebrated with Our Lady and sang the "Salve Regina." Then they said the rosary around the shrine, giving thanks especially to Little Mother and Mr. Jacoel.

Bishop O'Hara presided at the Pontifical Mass on July 16, and then processed into the garden with the assembled priests and deacons to bless the shrine to Mary. There was a hushed silence and collective awe as the Bishop blessed the statue. The Carmel of Buffalo now had a constant reminder that their Mother and Queen was with them always. To complete the shrine, however, the glass enclosure still had to be finished. Mother Rose contracted with a local Buffalo company for this work. Although Mr. Jacoel had donated both the statue and its base, the glass enclosure was not paid for. The Sisters prayed again to Our Lady and to Little Mother, and a short time later, Elizabeth Duffy, the sister of the former Bishop of Buffalo, donated the precise amount for the full glass enclosure. The company delivered it in the fall of 1951, and Bishop O'Hara once again came to bless the now fully encased statue on October 13. What a wonderful day! It was the close of the Holy Year and the anniversary of the Blessed Mother's last appearance at Fatima, where she held the Brown Scapular of Carmel in her hand. Little Mother's prayer for a life-sized statue of the Blessed Mother for the garden had come true.

Two years later on June 13, 1953, this story came full circle. Mother Rose, the Prioress, received a telegram from Laredo, Texas, from the Father William O'Connor, the Oblate Father whom Mr. Jacoel had originally consulted about the statue. Sadly, Fr. O'Connor reported that Mr. Jacoel had died that morning. He also reported something that the Sisters never could have foreseen—he baptized Mr. Jacoel a Catholic on his deathbed, at his insistence. Mother gathered all the Sisters around the shrine that Mr. Jacoel had donated to sing the Salve Regina. The inscription at the base of the statue read: "In loving memory of Mother Mary of St. John of the Cross, D.C., donated by Isidore Jacoel."

The souls of Mr. Jacoel and Little Mother, connected on earth, now shared a bond for eternity. A story of conversion and God's grace began with Mr. Jacoel's simple decision to reach out to the monastery. The Holy Spirit likely sparked Mr. Jacoel to do so, and the power of the Sisters' prayers guided the rest.

Another example was that of John Abramo, a kind benefactor who had often helped the Sisters repair garden equipment and fallen away from the Faith. The Sisters dutifully prayed for his return to the Church. One day Mr. Abramo was driving his truck when another driver negligently ran him off the road, and his car headed straight for a tree. Upon impact, Mr. Abramo miraculously saw a vision of Carmel sandwiched between the truck and the tree. He escaped from the vehicle without any bleeding, but he could not walk. After months in the hospital, and after hearing doctors' reports that he surely should have died, Mr. Abramo repented and wholeheartedly returned to the Faith. Embarrassed that perhaps no one would believe him, he confided in Sr. Mary Joseph, an Extern Sister. The Sisters rejoiced with gratitude to God for Mr. Abramo's return to the flock.

Both Mr. Jacoel's and Mr. Abramo's generosity and subsequent connection to the Carmelites of Buffalo are not just individual stories. They are testaments to the spiritual connectedness and impact that the monastery has beyond the cloister walls. God's graces flow from the monastery in many different shapes and forms. The end result might be a person finding the grace to forgive, or as awe inspiring as Mr. Abramo's near-death experience. Whether simple or profound, the events come about when souls connect in the Mystical Body of Christ. The Sisters live interior lives of prayer, but don't mistake their desire to retreat behind the cloister walls as a renunciation of mankind. The Carmelites renounce their desire to live in our world, but do not renounce those who live in it.

After Little Mother's death in 1949, the Carmel of Buffalo was blessed by the leadership of two very gifted Prioresses from 1949 to 1983, Mother Rose of the Immaculate Heart of Mary and Mother Mary Veronica of the Holy Face.[6] The first was born Mary Teresa Arabelle,

---

[6] Mother Mary Frances Teresa of the Infant Jesus & Holy Face did serve a period as Prioress from 1955 to 1958. She was also Prioress for two tenures while Little Mother was living, from 1933 to 1936 and 1942 to 1945. Mother Mary Frances Teresa was a

known to all as Belle Fox. Her family lived in Canada until hard times forced them to relocate to Buffalo. Belle was a religious child from the start, and she felt a vocation to the Carmel of Buffalo when she attended Easter Mass at the monastery in 1921. Sr. Rose of the Immaculate Heart of Mary entered Carmel in 1921, shortly after Mother Elias brought the Mexican Sisters from Grand Rapids. Mother Elias quickly recognized her virtue and appointed Sr. Rose as Novice Mistress soon thereafter. Sr. Rose held this position for the next twenty-five years. Her selfless devotion to the Community made her a natural choice for Prioress after Little Mother's death in 1949. Succeeding Little Mother was not easy, but Mother Rose combined humility with a generous fidelity to the Rule to ensure the monastery's continued vitality and development in the post-war years.

While the monastery maintained its steady presence in Buffalo, the world continued to change. The Second Vatican Council, in particular, wrought changes in Catholicism that were far reaching. Two events helped prepare the Community spiritually for the changes ahead. First, on May 17, 1952, the entire Community took Solemn Vows after the promulgation of the Apostolic Constitution *Sponsa Christi* by Pope Pius XII. Solemn Vows are the deepest consecration that the Religious can profess, but this privilege had been withdrawn by the Church in the aftermath of the French Revolution, as political instability and anti-clerical sentiment spread across Europe. *Sponsa Christi* restored this privilege, and the Carmelites of Buffalo, like many other Religious Orders, gratefully received this gift.

Second, shortly before the opening of Vatican II on October 11, 1962, the Carmel of Buffalo celebrated the fourth centenary of the founding of the Teresian Carmel. St. Teresa founded her first monastery in Avila, Spain, on the feast day of St. Bartholomew, August 24, 1562. Bishop Joseph Aloysius Burke joined the Sisters in 1962 to celebrate four centuries of the Discalced Carmelite Order and rejoice at how its monasteries had flourished throughout the world. The Carmel of Buffalo's ties to St. Teresa's first monastery in Avila remain strong to this day. The profession of Solemn Vows and the fourth centenary celebration were perfect preparation for the Carmel of Buffalo prior to

---

truly heroic and admirable woman whose fervor did much to build up the Carmel of Buffalo. Unfortunately, in the interests of brevity, we do not share her story here.

Vatican Council II. The Council ushered in considerable change in the Church, none of which will be debated here. But, although the Church may have changed dramatically, the Carmel of Buffalo did not. The key word being "dramatically." Rather, the monastery made changes consistent with Vatican II, while at the same time recommitting itself to its Teresian heritage, the Constitutions, and the Rule. The monastery emerged reinvigorated and stronger than ever.

The catalyst for the monastery's revival, amidst turmoil in the larger Church, was the guidance of Mother Mary Veronica of the Holy Face, who served as Prioress from 1964 to 1983. Jeannette Mary Voss was born on June 23, 1908. Both of her parents were deaf, and they met at St. Mary's School for the Deaf in Buffalo. Jeannette and her older brother Sidney never suffered from their parents' affliction and did not regard their parents' inability to hear as a handicap or hardship. Jeannette grew up with a keen sensitivity to the needs of others and a generous desire to be of service. At the age of five, with a five-cent piece in hand, she went to the most exclusive floral shop in Buffalo near her house and innocently asked the florist, while flashing her coin, to "give me the best you can for it's for my mother on Mother's Day." The florist, being a kind soul, proceeded to arrange a beautiful bouquet of roses, despite it costing well more than the five-cent piece. While Jeannette's mother was shocked and gratified at her daughter's resourcefulness and kindness, Jeannette saw nothing unusual in demanding that her mother have the best.

Jeannette attended Lafayette High School in Buffalo where she excelled artistically, scholastically, and socially. Tall and thin, she was good at sports, possessed a beautiful voice, and made friends easily. People wanted to follow her, and while she had many opportunities to make friends and date, she preferred to be with the group and enjoy everyone. Jeannette knew at a young age that she was called to the religious life, but there wasn't a particular Order that attracted her. She was aware of the Carmelite Monastery on Cottage Street because she often passed by, but she had never stopped to visit. Then, on Easter Day 1925, as Jeannette was enjoying a new book, her mother mentioned that she wanted to see the new Carmelite Monastery on Carmel Road. Never one to disappoint her mother, Jeannette sacrificed her desire to keep reading and agreed at once. When she stepped foot in the monastery chapel, she realized that it was indeed the Carmel of Buffalo where God was calling her. She was only seventeen, but soon applied.

On August 15, 1926, the Feast of the Assumption, Jeannette entered as an Extern Sister rather than a Cloistered Nun because of some confusion on the Chaplain's part. The Chaplain told Jeannette that the two vocations were essentially the same, and he thought that her gracious manner would be ideal for an Extern. But Jeannette longed for the cloister, and soon realizing the mistake, asked to be transferred. The Prioress regretfully told her that a change was not possible, and that she must remain an Extern. Resigned that this was God's will, she received the Holy Habit as an Extern in 1927 and professed first Vows in 1929. Then, some five years later, the Prioress, Mother Frances Teresa, summoned her. Mother told her that, if she still so desired, she could enter the cloister! Astonished, Sr. Mary Veronica of the Holy Face gladly accepted.

Sr. Veronica became a generous novice who gave herself completely to work and prayer. She thrived on it, and the Community soon recognized an untiring Sister with a vast array of talents. She could delicately paint, make lace, mix cement, cut down trees, and do just about everything else the monastery needed. Sr. Veronica was such a talented artist that she worked alongside Little Mother to portray the graphic sufferings of Christ on the hand-painted crucifixes. When Little Mother died in 1949, Sr. Veronica continued the Crucifix apostolate, but the supply of images to paint dwindled. Then, Sr. Veronica's brother, without knowing that the monastery had run short, told her that he had recently learned how to make molds and statues. In a short time, the monastery had a new supply of crucifixes to satisfy the pious desires of Carmel's patrons.

Tragedy struck Sr. Veronica's family in the summer of 1944, when a hit-and-run driver ran her father over and left him for dead. Looters stripped him of his possessions, and although an ambulance came, he eventually died from the injuries. Sr. Veronica's mother moved into a home run by the Franciscan Sisters, but only lived a few more years. Then most unexpectedly, Sister's only brother Sidney died of a heart attack after a business trip. Sister remained calm, composed, and silent during these trying times, despite the profound grief she must have experienced. It seemed that with each cross she threw herself with greater abandon into the Heart of Mary. Steadfast and true, Sr. Veronica possessed a strong will and natural leadership abilities.

It was no surprise that the Community elected her to the office of Prioress in 1964, during the Second Vatican Council in Rome. For the next twenty years, Mother Veronica guided the Community and provided the spiritual direction and nourishment necessary for its future. Mother Veronica undertook to carry out all the directives of the Council with a deep sense of humility. She sought advice from her superiors regarding the implementation of the Council's norms and all aspects of Carmelite life. She provided the Community with the Council documents so they could compare them with the requirements of the Carmelite Constitutions. Mother dedicated herself to this study with diligence and zeal, cataloguing all her findings in order to make a fervent defense of the Constitutions, which in some circles were coming into open discussion and debate.

The end result of this rigorous process was that Mother Veronica found new depth and beauty in the Teresian legislation, and she sought to preserve the Constitutions and spirit of the Carmelite Order. Through prayer, her example, and exhortations to the Community, Mother made clear that the Carmelite's Holy Mother, St. Teresa of Avila, would guide them through this time. Proclaimed a Doctor of the Church in 1970, St. Teresa provided the inspiration and nourishment that helped the Carmel of Buffalo stay true to its roots, while at the same time making necessary changes to fulfill recent directives of the Church. After making changes to the horarium (the daily schedule) and rubrics (instructions pertaining to the liturgy) required by the Council and directed by the Father General, the Sisters found themselves with an even deeper appreciation for the treasure inspired by their Holy Mother, St. Teresa.

Mother Mary Veronica of the Holy Face led both with a strong hand and great charity. She set the pace for the Community and protected it from harmful influences during turbulent times. She was not willing to make changes for the sake of change. Instead, she reexamined the Carmelite life after Vatican II, discerning what was consistent with the great tradition of the Carmelite Order. The Carmel of Buffalo adapted as needed but remained authentic in its living of the Carmelite charism. Carmel is akin to the desert to which Jesus often retreated to pray. Walls and grates mean nothing if everything can nevertheless enter. Just like St. Teresa of Avila envisioned, Mother let herself be fashioned into a strong stone building up the Community, and she ensured that her Sisters did the same.

During her first term as Prioress, Mother Veronica contracted a bad cold which developed into pneumonia, eventually leading to life-long asthma. In 1983, after stepping down as Prioress, various ailments came and went. She joyfully celebrated her Diamond Jubilee on August 15, 1986. Shortly before Christmas, however, Mother injured her back. Then, exposure to chemicals used to extinguish a fire on Christmas Eve seriously aggravated Mother's asthma. She died on January 21, 1987. A steady stream of people prayed before her mortal remains as she lay in state. Bishop Head celebrated her funeral, along with ten other priests and a Maronite Bishop. The Chapel overflowed with over two hundred people, and all sang the "Magnificat" at the end because Mother had said: "I expect to hear that as I go to Heaven." No greater tribute could be paid to Mother Veronica than the words of Father Silverio, a past Father General of the Order, as he concluded his work *The Perfect Carmelite*: "Here lies a Carmelite, who lived and gave the blood of her soul for the legislation and teachings of her Holy Parents."

The dedication of the Carmel of Buffalo's chapel was another noteworthy event in its history. Mother Mary St. Joseph of the Immaculate Conception succeeded Mother Veronica as Prioress in 1983. In 1990, her family donated the permanent marble Altar of Sacrifice, a precondition for the formal dedication along with retirement of the chapel debt. Bishop Head formally dedicated the chapel on December 14, 1991, the fourth centenary of St. John of the Cross's death, and he reminded the Sisters of their Founder's exhortation: "Sisters, let us be fervent, for it is the Lord we serve."

This ceremony marked the culmination of many years of hard work and the leadership of all the Prioresses, who prayed for the chapel's dedication. The following list includes all of the Carmel of Buffalo's Prioresses up to today:

1920-1923: Mother Mary Elias of the Most Blessed Sacrament

1923-1933: Mother Mary of St. John of the Cross

1933-1936: Mother Mary Frances Teresa of the Infant Jesus & the Holy Face

1936-1942: Mother Mary of St. John of the Cross

1942-1945: Mother Mary Frances Teresa of the Infant Jesus & the Holy Face

1945-1949: Mother Mary of St. John of the Cross

1949-1955: Mother Rose of the Immaculate Heart of Mary

1955-1958: Mother Mary Frances Teresa of the Infant Jesus & the Holy Face

1958-1964: Mother Rose of the Immaculate Heart of Mary

1964-1983: Mother Mary Veronica of the Holy Face

1983-1994: Mother Mary St. Joseph of the Immaculate Conception

1994-1997: Mother Marie Therese of the Child Jesus

1997-2018: Mother Miriam of Jesus

2018-Present: Mother Teresa of Jesus

As mentioned earlier, Carmel records its history in the Community chronicles. These accounts detail important events such as visits from the Father General or Prelates of the Church, as well as anniversaries and celebrations. Sometimes interesting events, such as the record rains that hit Buffalo on August 7, 1963, are described. Water filled the basement of the monastery and the Extern Sisters ventured into the flood to turn off the gas. Five feet of water filled the basement by the end of the day, flooding the storerooms and other parts of the monastery. The plumber came over with a pump to assist in getting the water out, but it was weeks before the monastery was cleaned and back to normal. The Sisters thanked God that no one was harmed.

Christmas Eve 1986 brought another surprise, when shortly before 8:00 p.m., as the Sisters were finishing preparations for Midnight Mass, some straw in the Nativity scene between the grates that separate the cloister choir from the sanctuary caught fire. Sr. Mary Joseph acted quickly, running to fetch a fire extinguisher and the other Externs to fight the fire. The flames were under control within five to ten minutes, but the smoldering continued. Mother called the Fire Department to ensure the fire was out, and Midnight Mass was cancelled since much clean-up was needed. The Sisters' quick actions impressed the Fire Chief, which in his opinion prevented a much worse catastrophe. He invited Sr. Marie Consolata and future Prioress, Mother Marie Therese, who fought the fire from opposite sides of the grate, to the Fireman's Ball to receive an award. Since the Carmelites do not attend social functions, a member of the Carmelite Secular Order went to accept the award on their behalf. Other significant events in the more recent history of the Carmel of the Little Flower of Jesus include the foundations made in Alexandria, South Dakota (1997) and Brooklyn, New York (2004), which have greatly blessed those local churches by the Sisters' hidden life of love and sacrifice.

Special mention must also be made of the Carmel of the Little Flower of Jesus's transition to the Extraordinary Form of the Mass or Tridentine Mass. As a growing number of Carmels have done in recent years, the Sisters embraced the traditional form of the liturgy, which is so well suited for their silent, contemplative life. To facilitate the offering of the Tridentine Mass, and as part of the Community's centenary celebration, the Sanctuary of the Chapel was restored in 2020 to its original beauty by Trabucco Design of Clarence, New York.

Although the interior life that each Sister lives may go unobserved by us, God sees all and rejoices. In turn, God sheds His grace on the Carmel of Buffalo and all those so fortunate to touch the monastery. The power of their prayers may be hidden, but as our world descends into a never-ending cacophony of "see me" pictures on Instagram, the Carmelite remains fixed on God. Therein lies the power of the monastery—to love God and implore Him to bestow His graces and love on all of us. Bishop James A. McNulty captured the power of Carmel in a sermon he delivered there on May 8, 1964, to celebrate the Silver Jubilee of three Sisters:

We are, indeed, so fortunate to have in our midst this powerhouse of prayer, of grace, of suffering, of magnificent works done by our good Sisters of Our Lady of Mount Carmel which are restricted by the walls of the convent ...

We are told that more is accomplished by prayer than we are aware of—and here within these blessed walls so much is accomplished for the Church, the Church universal as well as for the whole diocese of Buffalo ...

There are unusual ideas about the cloister. Some think that our Nuns are just escaping from the troubles of the world. Instead of that, they are the realists of the world. They remember our Lord's words, "Seek ye first the kingdom of God," the kingdom of Heaven, of justice. This is all they are doing, seeking the kingdom of God, and that is the solution of troubles.

What wisdom there is to live with God in this life in order to live with Him forever and ever—and that is the wisdom of the Carmelites. They want to be Christlike in life, and that is not just to be comfortable. They recognize in our beloved Savior the King of kings; that the Eternal Father has given Him title to every created gift; this from the moment of creation ...

Our Carmelites want to be Christlike. They had opportunities in the world; their own homes and their own families. And here in Carmel in their beautiful garden they understand the created gifts of God: they love to tend His growing things, His flowers, His fruits. But they are mindful that they came to the convent not for these things but rather to carry a cross, to make sacrifices, to pray and to suffer, for this is the divine strategy against sin; it is our Lord's weapon against sin.

> The faithful souls of Carmel love to carry a cross; it is not a dismal thing; it is a privileged thing because it brings them closer to Our Lord and enables them to resemble Him more closely.

The Carmelite acts out of a profound love for God. She leaves the world for the cloister, but she always desires to reach us. As Bishop McNulty said: "more is accomplished by prayer than we are aware of." We in society may not see it. As a result, we fail to comprehend the power of the Carmelites' prayers. But what if we acknowledged the Carmel of Buffalo's profound influence in the world—a distinct force for good? Just as a sailor who looks for a lighthouse in a storm, we too would see the monastery for what it is, a beacon calling us: "Come and hear, all ye that fear God, and I will declare what He hath done for my soul." (Psalm 66)

Mother Mary Veronica
of the Holy Face

Sr. Mary Joseph
of the Sacred Heart

Chapel Dedication December 14, 1991

Shrine to the Little Flower
(left of main altar)

**Shrine of Our Lady
of Mt. Carmel**

Ecce Homo Shrine
(back left of chapel)

**Sanctuary Chapel as
Restored in 2020**

The Cloister Garden

The Cloister Garden at Night

III
THE FRUITS OF THE GARDEN

7

The Love of Jesus Christ

My vocation is love!

St. Therese of Lisieux

Carmelites firmly believe in Christ's presence and not in the abstract sense either. Events often occur in daily life that cause the Sisters to say: "He is near!" The Sisters firmly believe that the Lord will provide, and He always does. For example, the monastery lives strictly on alms. Their abiding Faith sustains them. We, on the other hand, struggle to find God's presence in our lives. Many Catholics go to Mass and do not appreciate Christ's presence in the Eucharist. We look in the wrong places in hopes to find anything that satisfies, and we fail to find Him.

Christians naturally yearn for Christ. Augustine of Hippo described this yearning as: "Thou hast made us for thyself, O Lord, and our heart is restless until it finds its rest in thee." That yearning can be satisfied at the Carmel of Buffalo. Because the Carmelite's soul magnifies the Lord, they are filled with God's grace and the power of the Holy Spirit. The presence of God pervades the monastery; it is both palpable and unmistakable. We need only to quiet our minds and open our hearts to feel and recognize Him.

Against this backdrop, I first walked into the monastery in 1972, having just received my first Holy Communion as a second grader. Only seven years old, I had no profound sense of God, His presence in the Eucharist, or my Faith. The Carmelites changed that quickly.

As an altar boy, we wore black cassocks with white surplices. These vestments always were perfectly creased and squeaky clean. Indeed, the clean smell filled the whole monastery; like their Holy Mother St. Teresa, Carmelites love cleanliness. Walking out to serve Mass, pristine white linens, fresh flowers, and candles adorned the marble altar rising high to the blue ceiling which beckons the Queen of Carmel, Mary. Three large, wooden chairs sit to the right of the altar, closest to the black grate that shields the cloistered Sisters. As an altar boy, you learn early to look straight ahead and not into the cloister. On the wall opposite the black grate and in the Sisters' full view, three stained glass windows rise to the ceiling, with the Little Flower St. Therese and the Carmelites' Holy Father, St. John of the Cross, flanking the middle window of the Blessed Mother with Infant Jesus.

Turning to the nave, a walnut wood ceiling with wooden rafters extends horizontally across and gives the chapel an "old world" charm. Wooden pews line the church, and the choir loft sits at the back with organ pipes and another large, stained-glass window of the coronation of the Virgin Mary. Indeed, stained-glass windows surround the entire chapel on the bottom and top, each one dedicated to a particular saint. Statues flank each side of the sanctuary, with Our Lady to the left and St. Joseph and St. Teresa of Avila on the right. Most intriguing, there is a side altar on the left, appropriately hidden as a shrine to the Little Flower, and a hidden enclave in the back left of the chapel for the Ecce Homo shrine. Bright light filters into the pews on sunny days, and sound travels quickly and echoes throughout. The sounds of the Carmel of Buffalo compel the listener to pray, while at the same time disarm any fears or trepidation. When the the Sisters sing the lyrical Gregorian Chant, sound floats in the air, lingers, and softly penetrates the heart.

I had never heard voices like that. I loved my little world, playing at Shoshone Park and St. Rose of Lima, but the monastery was a world apart, from a time gone by when we held our Catholic Faith sacred and revered God in the Blessed Sacrament. Unlike the ebb and flow of Faith in society, the tide never receded at the monastery, slowing pulling you in. I wanted to serve Mass all the time, and particularly on Sundays, because Mass that day was not open to the public. While my family headed off to St. Rose, I felt special going to the monastery. The Sisters usually invited me to stay after for breakfast. Although I enjoyed the fresh fruit, bread, and pastries, it was the love with which the Sisters did everything that nourished my soul. The monastery started to feel like a spiritual "home."

As I entered my teenage years, my love for Carmel only increased, particularly around Holy Days. Christmas Midnight Mass was not open to the public, and at the time there wasn't just one Mass. The Carmelites had a High Mass, followed by what they called a Shepherds' Mass because the appointed reading recounted when the shepherds found

Mary, Joseph, and the Infant. Leaving the monastery early Christmas morning around 2:30 a.m., often with fresh snow fallen, it felt like Bethlehem to this young Buffalo boy.

I also started to appreciate more the women called to this life. First, I noticed the distinctive way Carmelites speak and carry themselves. Thoughtful in their words, the Sisters possess a unique ability to edify their listeners and sanctify any topic. Second, I learned cloistered Sisters never leave the monastery, unless for medical or other serious reasons. That seemed quite radical, and at the same time impressive. Finally, I sensed these women were far more attuned to God's presence. I couldn't confirm that any Sister had fully climbed Mount Carmel and spoke with God, but I didn't know anyone else who had gotten as close.

After the countless Masses, the Sisters and everything about the monastery touched my soul. I started to listen, really listen, amidst the silence. God and faith in God became real at the Carmel of Buffalo because of the Sisters and God's presence.

I left Buffalo in 1983 to attend the U.S. Naval Academy. Time flew by as I married Susan upon graduation and started a series of Marine Corps deployments to Europe, Liberia, and the Gulf War. I rarely spoke with Susan when deployed, including for months when she was pregnant with our first child. But the Marine Corps always did a good job to ensure Catholics could attend Mass, unless it wasn't safe. At Mass, my mind drifted to that "better place," which always included just two things, Susan and the Carmel of Buffalo. I heard the Sisters and felt the tug of the monastery calling me home.

This longing for the monastery made little sense to me. Buffalo wasn't home anymore. I had never spoken with a cloister Sister. And yet, these Carmelites still reached me years later, separated by thousands of miles. I had spent countless hours in their midst as a boy, but why had the Sisters stayed with me?

In discussions with the Carmelites of Buffalo to write this book, a Sister said to me, "Carmel is a privileged place where the soul is freed to encounter Christ in a profound way." That explained my deep bond with Carmel years after leaving Buffalo. I longed for the monastery because there I found Christ—in the chapel, in the silence, and most of all in the Sisters. Thomas Merton wrote in *New Seeds of Contemplation* that: "Every moment and every event of every man's life on earth plants something in his soul." All those moments at the monastery had indeed planted something in my soul—a profound sense of Christ in me, my life, and my fellow man.

A Fruit of the Garden is Christ's presence. The Carmelites bring Christ to the world. Come and experience Christ in the chapel. Attend Mass and listen to the Carmelites in song. In addition to Holy Days and regular daily Mass, the Carmel of Buffalo celebrates a Triduum throughout the year, for St. Joseph in March, Our Lady of Mt. Carmel (Mary) in July, and St. Therese the Little Flower in October. A Triduum usually entails nightly Mass for three consecutive days, with a sermon and special prayers. I always served Mass for this celebration, and much to my surprise, women can be quite forceful when it comes to getting roses from the Carmel of Buffalo.

Another way to experience the chapel is to visit outside of Mass. A Carmelite of Buffalo described Carmel as "God's Embassy on Earth." Just visit and be in Christ's presence. Whether seeking an escape from the noise, or during a time of need, the monastery provides respite. When Bishop Turner laid the cornerstone for the chapel in September 1924, here was the scene:

> Despite the threatening clouds, fully five thousand people gathered near the foundations of the new edifice to take part in the dedication. Seats had been arranged in front of the canopy of Bishop William Turner, but long before the ceremonies began it was found that these could not accommodate the throng. Police were kept busy before the arrival of Bishop Turner and the procession in keeping the large crowd from the platform.

Five thousand people gathering at the Carmel of Buffalo does not seem possible today. But St. Therese's "Little Way" teaches us that we should take that first little step. With just one step, you can and will feel Christ in your life.

***

Sr. Mary Joseph had the face of Jesus Christ.

An Extern Sister from 1954 to 2003, she served as the face of the Carmel of Buffalo for fifty years. She exemplified the Carmelites' ability to bring Christ's love to others and to sacrifice so that God may shed His grace on us. St. Teresa of Calcutta serves as perhaps the best modern-day example of bringing Christ to others. Before she could bring Christ to the poor of Calcutta, however, Mother Teresa had to fill her heart with Christ's love.

A young priest named Father Angelo Comastri came to Calcutta one day with the sole purpose of meeting Mother Teresa. But when he asked at the convent to meet her, the Sister at the door said: "I am sorry! That is not possible!" Fr. Comastri persisted and said that he would not leave until meeting her. Some time passed and the Sister returned with Mother Teresa. The priest confided in Mother Teresa that he was young, just starting out, and wanted to have Mother Teresa's prayers. She responded: "I always pray for priests. I will pray for you also." She also gave the priest a miraculous medal and asked: "For how much time do you pray each day?" A bit surprised, Fr. Comastri said: "Mother, I celebrate Holy Mass each day, I pray the Breviary each day … I pray the rosary each day also and very gladly because I learned it from my mother." Mother Teresa paused and with her hands clasping her rosary said: "That is not enough, my son! That is not enough, because love demands the maximum!"

Now embarrassed and without fully understanding Mother Teresa's words, he asked: "Mother, I expected from you instead this question: What acts of charity do you do?" Mother Teresa became very serious again and said: "Do you think that I could practice charity if I did not ask Jesus every day to fill my heart with His love? Do you think I could go through the streets looking for the poor if Jesus did not communicate the fire of His charity to my heart?" And the priest, feeling rather small in Mother Teresa's presence, realized he had fallen short. Mother Teresa gently guided him: "Read the Gospel attentively, and you will see that Jesus sacrificed even charity for prayer. And do you know why? To teach us that, without God, we are too poor to help the poor!"

The Carmelites fill their lives with prayer to fill their souls with God. Like Mother Teresa, only then can they share Christ with others. The Sisters seek to share Christ with us through the raw power of prayer and the intercession of the Saints. They hope that we will recognize Him and feel His love.

As an Extern Sister, Sr. Mary Joseph greeted, listened to, consoled, and touched thousands. We learn at a young age to see Christ in others, and then we find that lesson can be hard to apply. Sr. Mary Joseph mastered that lesson. God gave her a gift to reach people with love, and she pursued her Carmelite vocation to perfect that gift. All those that ever met her can attest to Sr. Mary Joseph's unique talents. She was a true missionary and exemplified the Carmel of Buffalo's desire to bring Christ to others.

Born Jane Elizabeth Miller in Omaha, Nebraska on May 31, 1912, her family moved back to Buffalo when she was young. Jane often helped her mother in their greeting card store on Hertel Avenue, the Miriam Shop. Likely there, her flair for conversation blossomed. Jane was quite close to her brother Paul, whom she found one day with a friend shooting a BB gun at Coke bottles on a fence. As they struggled to hit the targets, Jane watched and asked for a turn. She aimed and easily hit the Coke bottles with successive shots. When the boys seemed surprised, Jane looked at them as if to say: "But of course I hit the target ... What did you expect?" Jane remained close to Paul as he married and had children. She would often take her nieces and nephews to Kleinhans Music Hall for performances. She made her own clothes and dressed fashionably. She also decorated Chinese figurines and designed her own Christmas cards. Indeed, with her grace, talents, and charm, Jane Miller's personality resembled accounts given of the Carmelite's founder, St. Teresa of Avila, before she joined the monastery.

Jane graduated from Bennett High School and completed a business course at the Chown School of Business in 1930. She became a legal stenographer for Cotter and Hillery, and then served as an assistant secretary to the Chancellor of the University of Buffalo from 1932 to 1942, where she audited English courses in addition to her work. She joined the U.S. Naval Reserve in December 1942 as a "Wave," and served in Washington D.C. at the Bureau of Aeronautics.

Jane attained the rank of Lieutenant Junior Grade and was always proud of her military service. After the war, she returned to the University of Buffalo as secretary to the Chancellor again. Around this time, Jane joined the Third Order of Carmel and received as patroness St. Teresa Margaret of the Heart of Jesus, an Italian Carmelite characterized best by her hiddenness. Although it might seem ironic that someone as outgoing as Jane would receive as patroness a saint whose characteristic trait was hiddenness, the match fit perfectly because she soon found St. Teresa Margaret asking her to give up everything to become a Carmelite of Buffalo.

She entered the Community as an Extern Sister on the feast of St. Joseph, March 19, 1954. She always described her call to Carmel in a simple, yet grand style: "There I was, sitting on the davenport, talking on the phone, when it hit me like a lightning bolt … A Carmelite Extern Sister!" She quit her work promptly and told them "I'm going into business for myself." One year after entrance, she received the Holy Habit and her Religious name, Sr. Mary Joseph of the Sacred Heart. She made her first Vows in August 1957 and Final Profession in September 1962. Her indomitable spirit had a lasting impact on the Carmel of Buffalo. Sr. Mary Joseph displayed limitless generosity of heart, a charming simplicity, and incomparable obedience to her superiors. She fulfilled all of her duties with diligence and precision, qualities that she attributed to her naval service. An avid gardener, passersby would often see Sr. Mary Joseph tending to the grounds in the Extern Sisters' yard, even into her mid-80s. One day while weeding a flower bed, a little boy across the street asked: "Sister, can you come over and play?" Much to the boy's surprise, Sr. Mary Joseph many decades his senior replied: "I have to ask my Mother first!" She was never at a loss for what to say or how to say it.

Sister trained the altar boys at the Carmel of Buffalo for many years. For every Mass, and especially on major feast days, she prearranged and scripted everything with precision and detail. Altar boys, lectors, and anyone with a role in Mass at Carmel knew who was in charge, and they also knew that Sr. Mary Joseph demanded perfection. Although she readily understood that her standard might be high, she instilled in all a sincere desire to reach it nonetheless. Her organizational skills rivaled any battle plan at the Pentagon, and the end result was always a beautiful Mass, one that gave glory to God. Sr.

Mary Joseph would be the last to take credit, but everyone knew that she made Mass at the Carmel of Buffalo special.

Sr. Mary Joseph also had a great devotion to the Holy Face of Jesus. Mother Rose and Mother Mary Frances Teresa wanted to establish the Confraternity of the Holy Face at the monastery in the 1950s, in particular because of the rapid growth of Communism. Bishop Joseph A. Burke canonically erected the Confraternity at the Carmel of Buffalo on July 7, 1960, with the purpose of paying homage to and increasing love for the Holy Face and for God's mercy on Communists. The Community worked with clergy to compile the "Little Manual of the Confraternity of the Holy Face," which is still available at the Carmel of Buffalo today. When Benediction of the Most Blessed Sacrament is celebrated at Carmel, the priest and congregation recite the prayer for the conversion of the Communists and other prayers in honor of the Holy Face.

Sr. Mary Joseph worked tirelessly to increase enrollment in the Confraternity throughout her years at Carmel. She had an earnest desire for people to make reparation for any offenses against God's Holy Name. She also promoted other Carmelite devotions such as distributing blessed rose petals to patrons in honor of Saint Therese and holy water blessed with the relic of Saint Albert of Trapani. She knew countless stories of people who had received special blessings after using "Saint Albert's water." God alone knows how many souls Sr. Mary Joseph touched and how many lives she changed. Never one to draw attention to herself, Sr. Mary Joseph would smile and deflect credit for all her wondrous deeds.

I met Sr. Mary Joseph in 1972. Her face remains firmly etched in my mind decades later. The Holy Habit of Carmel accentuates a Carmelite's face.

I learned over my many years as an altar boy that, while she could be stern at times, Sr. Mary Joseph genuinely cared for everyone she met. Her warm personality and intellect made everyone that met her feel special. Confident and determined, she had a commanding presence. Like a true leader, she led by example. Before Mass, altar boys wait in a small room, sitting on little, wooden stools. Despite being busy with preparations for Mass, Sr. Mary Joseph always took time to ask how you were doing. She had a quick wit and invariably made me laugh. Although kind in every action, she was not afraid to point out my mistakes after Mass. She challenged me to do better. My brother Dan and I often served Mass together, and Sr. Mary Joseph made sure for important feasts that both "Danny" (as she referred to my brother) and I were available.

Dan left Buffalo in 1979 for the U.S. Naval Academy. Sr. Mary Joseph, as a former naval officer, beamed. I continued as an altar boy through my high school years. It was now just Sundays and major feast days, because weekday Mass conflicted with school. As my days at Carmel grew less frequent, I noticed that Mass elsewhere seemed different. The Carmel of Buffalo provided a deep peace and beauty missing elsewhere. I started to appreciate my visits to Carmel even more. The room and wooden stools seemed much smaller, and when Sr. Mary Joseph stopped by to chat before Mass, the conversation changed. Having gotten quite good as an altar boy, she wanted me to strive for perfection in every endeavor—school, athletics, and most of all Faith.

She told me to pray, always pray!

Sr. Mary Joseph said she and her Sisters would pray for me and my family. Each time she did, humility overcame me. All I ever did was show up to serve Mass. Most of the Sisters I had never met. I wasn't deserving of their prayers. But none of that mattered. And after a chat with Sr. Mary Joseph, Mass provided the opportunity to become lost in the beauty of Carmel all over again. But then I, too, left Buffalo for the Naval Academy, and Sr. Mary Joseph beamed once more. She had good reason to take credit for the Valaik boys' desire to join the military, because she certainly taught us the value of service, discipline, and attention to detail.

In her later years, Sr. Mary Joseph's health declined. She suffered a fall in early 1995 and a severe bout of the flu in 2000. In characteristic fashion, after being close to death in 2000, she commented: "I'm afraid I'm going to *live!*" Her wit never faded. She suffered a few heart attacks and a severe broken leg in 2002, but she also saw the fulfillment of a long-cherished hope that year when the monastery completed the revised manual of the Confraternity of the Holy Face with the help of

91

Father Paul J. McDonald. Carmel's faithful friend and benefactor, Vinny Philippone, who so generously printed copies of Veronica's veil with cards, also generously assisted in the Holy Face apostolate.

Sr. Mary Joseph died on March 22, 2003, surrounded by her Sisters and fingering her rosary beads. Just prior to her death, Sister asked pardon for any failings and prayed for the intentions of peace, for our president, and the members of the armed forces. A faithful servant to her God, her Sisters, and her country, Sr. Mary Joseph fulfilled her vocation and God's will.

Years after leaving Buffalo it dawned on me that Sr. Mary Joseph had the face of Christ because she embodied His Love. Carmel's love manifested itself to me in Sr. Mary Joseph. With her unique spirit, Sr. Mary Joseph taught the altar boys St. Therese's "Little Way." Strive to be good altar boys; seek perfection in every little task; and, do all things with great love. Sr. Mary Joseph didn't just train good altar boys; she trained boys to be men of Christ.

The Carmelites seek Christ first of all to satisfy their unquenchable desire for Him and fill their hearts with Him. But the Carmelite's goal is not just to find Christ, but in doing so to atone for our sins, to convert sinners, lift up those who are suffering, and to bring Christ's love to others. Since God becomes the goal, death brings the longed-for vision of her Beloved. St. Teresa of Avila captured the grace that a Carmelite receives in *The Way of Perfection*:

> It is no surprise that those who have a share in the consolations of God desire to be there where they will enjoy them more than in mere sips, that they do not want to remain in a life where there are these many obstacles to the enjoyment of so much good, and that they desire be where the Sun of Justice does not set.... Oh, how different this life would have to be in order for one not to desire death! How our will deviates in its inclination from that which is the will of God. He wants us to love truth; we love the lie. He wants us to desire the eternal; we here below, lean toward what comes to an end. He wants us to desire sublime and great

things; we, here below, desire base and earthly things.

The greatest Fruit of the Garden is Christ's love. As seen in the life of Sr. Mary Joseph, the Carmelite vocation embodies a wholehearted gift of oneself for others. St. Therese wrote: "My vocation is love!" That is the Carmelite's life and vocation.

**

How many people over the years have driven or walked by 75 Carmel Road and asked: "What do those nuns do all day?"

The Carmelites of Buffalo shun attention or serious inquiry as to what they do and why they do it. A natural "détente" results between the monastery and the larger world around it, where neither side disturbs the other. While that makes sense, because the monastery remains wrapped in mystery, the casual observer does not understand what a vital role this institution plays. Similar to the Marine standing post in some far-flung location to protect our freedoms, we take the Sisters and their sacrifices for granted. We shouldn't.

My hope is that the Carmelites of Buffalo and their vocations have become more understandable here, and that mutual gratitude remains a Fruit of the Garden and grows even stronger. To understand what they do and why they do it should inspire us. At a minimum, we should appreciate these dedicated lives as a living example of Christ's love.

But more than that, we lay people need to work harder to bridge the gap between the monastery and our world. Come visit the Carmel of Buffalo, pray, sacrifice, and love as the Carmelites do. Only then will we start to see the connection between the monastery and our world. Only then will we too draw closer to God and fill our hearts with His love. And only then will it be possible to see people through a new lens—where love creates the different hues, and we see that "every flower created by Him is beautiful," as St. Therese encouraged us. Although ambitious, that is my hope and what the Carmel of Buffalo works for each day.

Whether or not we achieve this goal, please consider doing a few more things as the monastery turns one hundred. First, stop and celebrate. Salute the Sisters' steadfast commitment to build a monastery in north Buffalo and sustain it for a century. Celebrate Mother Elias's courage and vision and Little Mother's leadership during the early years. Acknowledge and be grateful for all the Sisters who have dedicated their lives to keep this light burning. Not every city has a Carmelite monastery, but Buffalo has that great fortune. Appreciate the Beautiful Garden and how much it adds to our wonderful city.

Second, draw closer to the beauty of the Carmel of Buffalo. The beauty lies in the fact that Christ dwells in the Sisters' souls, as St. John of the Cross so aptly described:

> O soul, most beautiful of creatures, who desires so ardently to know the dwelling place of your Beloved in order to seek Him and be united with Him, you are yourself the refuge where He takes shelter, the dwelling place in which He hides Himself. Your Beloved, your Treasure, your one Hope is so close to you as to live within you; and, actually you cannot have life without Him!

St. Elizabeth of the Trinity commented on this passage: "That is the whole life of Carmel, to live in Him. Then all sacrifices, all immolations become divine, for through everything that soul sees Him whom it loves, and everything leads it to Him; it is a continual heart-to-heart!" We are naturally attracted to beautiful things, whether it be found in nature, art, or love. So too should we be attracted to the Carmel of Buffalo.

Finally, learn from the Sisters that Faith lived vibrantly and authentically is the only choice. A Carmelite of Buffalo said: "We live with our sights set on Heaven, with joyful hope in the glorious Life that awaits us." A simple statement, but one with profound implications if believed. Carmelites never say "look at us." But we should and feel a deep sense of gratitude because the monastery provides a real-life example of Faith lived to the fullest. God does not call everyone to Carmel, but He does call all of us to live our Faith with zeal. So, seek Him with all your heart.

My gratitude to the Sisters remains overwhelming almost fifty years after meeting them as a young boy. Along with Buffalo's gratitude to the Carmel of Buffalo, the Sisters' gratitude to the Buffalo community, its neighbors, benefactors, and friends remains overwhelming as well.

***

It is a profound joy and privilege to have this opportunity to greet our many faithful friends and benefactors, both near and far! On behalf of all the Sisters, I would like to thank you from the bottom of my heart for all your generosity to this Monastery of the Little Flower of Jesus. Without your gracious support, it would not be possible for us to live our hidden life of love and sacrifice in the heart of the Church. Your faith in the power of prayer, most especially in the intercessory power of our patroness Saint Therese of the Child Jesus, is truly an inspiration to us, encouraging us to give ourselves with ever greater generosity to our contemplative vocation.

Over the past century, Saint Therese has worked miracles of grace for those who have reached out to us to invoke her aid. Not long before the saint's death, her sisters asked, "You will look down on us from heaven, won't you?" and she eagerly responded, "NO!... I will COME DOWN!" How often people have felt her presence in our chapel, the first dedicated to her as a canonized Saint! Indeed, Saint Therese has "come down" on so many occasions and in so many ways! With heartfelt fervor, we especially ask her to intercede for the Diocese of Buffalo, whose faithful have been so devoted to this Monastery over the past hundred years. May she "let fall a shower of roses" on the good people of this Diocese, bringing peace, healing, and a renewal of genuine and joyful Catholic faith and devotion.

To all who contact us with your prayer petitions, thank you for entrusting to us the intentions so dear to your hearts! Your needs are ours, and we are honored to bring you and your loved ones to the Lord each day in prayer. A Carmelite is called to be a mother of souls, and we take this obligation of love very seriously. How beautiful is this unity we share in the Mystical Body of Christ! May God reward you with His choicest graces and blessings for all of the support you have given to the Monastery over the years! United with all the saintly Sisters who have gone before us, who now intercede for our friends and benefactors before the throne of God, we remember you in prayer each day with hearts full of gratitude. God bless you!!

> *Mother Teresa of Jesus, OCD*
> *Prioress of The Carmel of Buffalo*

About the Author

Michael Valaik grew up in Buffalo, New York and attended St. Joseph's Collegiate Institute. He graduated with honors from the United States Naval Academy in Annapolis, Maryland in 1988. That same year he earned a M.A. in Modern Military History from the University of Maryland, writing his Thesis on *Winston Churchill and the Naval Estimates Crises of 1909 and 1914*. As a Marine Corps Officer, Mike led Marines in the evacuation of 4,000 people from the Liberian Civil War in Operation Sharp Edge (1990) and led Marines in the ground combat offensive against Iraqi enemy forces in Operation Desert Storm (1991). He then earned his Juris Doctor degree at night from Georgetown University Law School in 1996 and exited the Marine Corps. For the last twenty-four years, Mike has tried cases throughout the United States, and he is also an Adjunct Professor of Law at Northwestern Law School.

In 1972, Mike became an altar boy at the Carmel of Buffalo. His connection to the Carmelites remains strong to this day. Mike lives in Chicago with his wife Susan.

CPSIA information can be obtained
at www.ICGtesting.com
Printed in the USA
BVHW060039300322
632824BV00009B/597